A DOG OWNER'S GUIDE TO

LABRADOR RETRIEVERS

Tetra⊙Press

No. 16029

A DOG OWNER'S GUIDE TO

LABRADOR RETRIEVERS

Marjorie Satterthwaite

Photographs by Marc Henrie

A Salamander Book

© 1987 Salamander Books Ltd.,
Published in the USA by Tetra Press
3001 Commerce Street, Blacksburg, VA 24060

ISBN 1-56465-134-7

Library of Congress number: 87-050047

This book may not be sold outside the
United States of America and Canada

All correspondence concerning the content of this volume
should be addressed to Tetra Press.

Credits

Editor: Jo Finnis
Designers: Glynis Edwards; Philip Gorton
Photographs: Marc Henrie, Gerard Van Klaveren;
Andy Blower; Robert Smith; S & G Agency Ltd
Illustrations: Ray Hutchins; Clive Spong
Color origination: Rodney Howe Ltd;
Contemporary Lithoplates Ltd
Typesetting: The Old Mill
Printed in Belgium

Contents

Author

Marjorie Satterthwaite has been breeding Labrador Retrievers for over 25 years, and many have become champions all over the world. She bred the first every English male chocolate Labrador champion, Hot Chocolate, which went to the United States of America some seven years ago, becoming a Champion there also.
In addition to Labradors, Marjorie also breeds English Springer Spaniels and Golden Retrievers, and has bred many champions.
Marjorie is an international judge — in Europe, New Zealand, Australia, Kenya and the USA. She is qualified to judge four breeds in the gundog group — English Springer Spaniels, Labrador Retrievers, Golden Retrievers and Irish Water Spaniels — as well as the gundog group itself. Marjorie judged the Labrador Retrievers at Crufts Dog Show in 1980.

Contributor

Keith Butt, MA, VetMB(Cantab), MRCVS has contributed the chapter on veterinary care. Keith qualified in 1961 at Cambridge University. He runs his own veterinary practice in Kensington, London, and is himself a breeder and owner of many different breeds of pedigree dogs.

US consultant

Hal Sundstrom, as president of Halamar Inc, publishers of North Virginia, has been editing and publishing magazines on travel and pure-bred dogs since 1972. He is the recipient of six national writing and public excellence awards from the Dog Writer's Association of America, of which he is now president, and he is a past member of the Collie Club of America. He is now a delegate to the American Kennel Club representing the Collie Club of America.
Hal has an extensive background and enormous experience in the dog world as a breeder/handler/exhibitor, match and sweeps judge, officer and director of specialty and all-breed clubs, show and symposium chairman, and officer of the Arizona and Hawaii Councils of Dog Clubs.

Photographer

Marc Henrie began his career as a Stills Man at the famous Ealing Film Studios in London. He then moved to Hollywood where he worked for MGM, RKO, Paramount and Warner Brothers, photographing the Hollywood greats: Humphrey Bogart, Edward G Robinson, Gary Cooper, Joan Crawford and Ingrid Bergman, to name a few. He was one of the last photographers to photograph Marilyn Monroe. During this time, he was in great demand to photograph the stars with their pets.
Later, after he had returned to England, Marc specialized in photographing dogs and cats, rapidly establishing an international reputation.
He has won numerous photographic awards, most recently the Kodak Award for the Best Animal Photograph and the Neal Foundation Award for Outstanding Photography of Animal Behaviour.
Marc is married to ex-ballet dancer, Fiona Henrie, who now writes and illustrates books on animals. They live in West London with their daughter Fleur, two Cavalier King Charles Spaniels and a cat called Topaz.

Author's acknowledgements

The author wishes to thank Marianne and Janet Coffman for word-processing the manuscript; Mrs Montgomery Charrington for assisting with photographs of gundogs and gundog training; Dick and Marilyn Reynolds (Judge: Peggy Rae) for supplying their photograph of an American show; Barry Stocks for the text on Guide Dogs for the Blind; E. Jackie Ransom for text and illustrations in the History chapter.

Introduction

Is a Labrador for you?

To decide whether or not the Labrador, out of the many breeds of dog available, is the sort of dog you would care to own as a companion, it is helpful to go through a checklist of very specific considerations. This must include the size of the animal, its adaptability, the amount of care it requires including grooming and exercise, the size of your own home and garden, how much time each member of the family is going to devote to the dog — not just whilst it is in its lovable, cuddly stage, but in the years ahead. A substantial amount of time will also be needed to train the dog to take its part as yet another member of the family.

You must remember, also, that owning a dog involves a wider responsibility, to the outside world — your immediate neighbours and the general public — for good behaviour in all situations.

The Labrador puppy

The owner or potential owner of a small, cuddly, roly-poly Labrador puppy, inevitably attracting attention for its friendliness and good looks, must be well aware that it is going to grow into a big, friendly dog, always wanting to please and be a constant companion to all the family. The Labrador puppy will grow to adore exercise, especially long country walks where it can use all its natural instincts of scenting rabbits and hare, pheasant, partridge and duck. The Labrador has a great love of water in any form, be it the muddiest pool or swift-flowing river — but never a bath! At home, the Labrador loves to play seeking and fetching with a ball, and will always be ready to pick up absolutely anything — but particularly food!

To reach maturity, the Labrador has to go through many days, weeks and months of puppyhood. During waking hours, as the puppy grows, it will spend its time dashing about the home, grabbing in its mouth any small, household object in its wake. The Labrador puppy is not adverse to children's toys — and here the owner must be very careful to hide dangerous objects, particularly plastic ones.

As the Labrador grows, it will discover that there is more to life than

floors and chairs — there are worktops where food is being prepared. There is nothing quite so delicious to a Labrador than a piece of freshly-roasted meat, and in the dog's terms, it is simply retrieving it for the family!

The mature Labrador

Being classified as a gundog (or sporting dog in the USA), the Labrador enjoys both routine and exercise in any weather, and a good warm bed, good food and companionship is all its asks for. A bed of its own is very important — a place where the dog can get away from it all, or hide after it has splattered mud all over the kitchen doors with its tail and all over the floor with its muddy paws. Beware the low coffee table where its happily-wagging tail can lay to waste mugs or cups and saucers.

Outside, the Labrador must be contained — nothing less than a 6-foot (2-metre) stout fence. Anything lower will be viewed with contempt. The Labrador is a great gardener, particularly in the Spring, when it will endeavour re-arrange your neatly-planted bulbs, scuffle through rows of newly-set seeds, or cavort around the garden with a daffodil or two neatly carried in its mouth.

Unlike children, a dog cannot really comprehend your language. So, perhaps to begin with, your Labrador is going to be a little more difficult to bring up than a child, because of the limited means of communication — it cannot talk and can only understand a few words, and recognize extremes of tone in your voice. But given lots of time, patience, company and discipline, your Labrador will grow to be an ideal companion — both in the home and out in the country too. It will not answer you back, just repay you many times over with its love of life.

Below left: A dog that loves fun and games with people or other animals, the Labrador makes an ideal family companion.

Below: A Labrador enjoying a combination of its two favourite pastimes — paddling or swimming in water and retrieving an object.

Chapter One

A HISTORY OF THE LABRADOR

Nineteenth century ancestors
Yellows
Chocolates
Sandylands Kennel
The United States

ORIGINS

Nineteenth century ancestors

Labradors in England were first recognized by the Kennel Club in 1904, but almost a century before fishermen in Greenland were using a very similar dog for retrieving fish. Later the dogs were to be found travelling on fishermen's boats between Newfoundland and England.

There seems to have been two distinct types — the larger with a heavy black coat, known as a Newfoundland, and the smaller variety which was more agile, known as the St. John's dog. Their coats were very thick and impervious to water, with a short, thick tail rounded like an otter's. This was the dog that figured in earlier writings, and is generally believed to be the ancestor of today's Labrador.

Once the dog settled in England, game-shooting sportsmen were quick to realize its assets. Not only would it catch and retrieve fish, but it would retrieve shot duck from water and game on land.

As early as 1870, in an article on Prize Dogs at the Birmingham Show which appeared in the *Illustrated London News* on 10 December, the following comment was made on the Newfoundland Dogs which had

Below: *An 1872 engraving of Billy a St John's or lesser Labrador. Billy's breeder saw him as a 'pure, small Labrador', but his coat is too curly for a pure-bred dog today.*

Bottom: *Leo, a Newfoundland born in 1872 and bred by W Coates, was a superb specimen and won many first prizes, in spite of the brownish tinge to his coat.*

been shown there: 'We should like to see them divided into two Classes, the Newfoundland so well known, and the Coal Black Labrador which is a separate breed.'

The Hon A Holland Hibbert, later Viscount Knutsford, is thought to be the first breeder of Labradors in the UK, having commenced breeding true to type in 1884. In 1904 his Munden Single became the first Labrador to run in Field Trials. In 1905 Munden Sentry won the Dog Challenge Certificate at the Crystal Palace Kennel Club Show, and the Certificate of Merit at the International Gun Dog League Retriever Trials.

Another famous Labrador was M Portal's FT Champion Flapper, bred by Colonel Bates, born 1902 (a progeny of Munden Sybil, 1884), whose influence at stud was considerable and a winner of many Field Trials in 1904-8.

1909 saw the debut of Field Trial Champion Peter of Faskally bred by G Watson, born February 1908, owned by H E Butler and sired by Waterdale Gamester Ex Nell. Peter's pedigree also goes back to the Munden line of Holland Hibbert.

Peter was used extensively at stud, and one of his sons in the background of today's Labrador was Ch Withington Dorando, born 1912, bred by T Parmley. When owned by J T Hulmes, in 1913 Dorando won several Trials and by 1914 he had passed into the ownership of Captain and Mrs Quintin Dick (later Lorna, Countess Howe). They exhibited him at many shows and trials, and in 1915 he obtained the title of Show Champion while continuing to win at many Field Trials.

Captain and Mrs Dick's first Labrador was a male, bred by Lord Vivian, Scandal of Glyn born 1914. A son of Scandal mated to Caerhowell Nettle, bred by Major H Banner, became the first Dual Champion, Banchory Bolo, originally registered as Caerhowell Bully (born 29 December 1915).

Below: *Ch and FT Ch Bramshaw Bob was born on 11 December 1929, sired by Ch Inglestone Ben ex Bramshaw Brimble. He was owned and shown by Lorna, Countess Howe, and won Best in Show at Crufts in 1932 and 1933, and many other prizes besides.*

A kennel which did much for the breed was that of Mr H A Saunders. His first champion, Ch Tar of Hamyax born in August 1914 and sired by Toi of Whitmore Ex Sunshine of Yaxham, with a bitch called Rockstead Swift, appear to be the foundation stock of the very successful Liddly Labradors.

The popularity of the Labrador both in Field Trials and in the show ring continued to rise. The breed won Best in Show at Crufts on three occasions: Lady Howe's Ch Bramshaw Bob, at his first show, won this award two years in succession — 1932 and 1933; four years later Lady Howe again won this presitigious award with Ch Cheverella Ben of Banchory.

At Crufts in 1938, HM King George VI exhibited a Labrador, Sandringham Stream, born 1934, bred by HM King George V and sired by Ch Banchory Truman Ex Sandringham Swim.

Yellows
The first appearance of a Yellow Labrador dates back to 1899 when Major C Radclyffe bred two Yellows from Black parentage, Ben of Hyde, a name in most pedigrees of the past. The Labrador Club was founded in 1916, and although Blacks predominated in the breed at this time, the Yellows began to be recognized as well.

Mrs. Veronica Wormald persisted in breeding a dual-purpose Yellow and founded the Yellow Labrador Club in 1925. She continued field trialling and showing her Labradors until very late in her life, and I can remember walking up at a field trial with her when she was well into her eighties — and many of us can remember her exhibiting at Crufts as late as 1978.

Chocolates
The third colour in Labradors is Chocolate, and Mrs Pauling and Mr Severn bred some lovely dogs of this colour — then called liver — but it was to Mrs Pauling that the honour came of breeding the first Chocolate champion bitch Ch Cookridge Tango. Even today, we only have

Below: *Ch Chevrelle Ben of Banchory, born 5 August 1933, sired by Ch Inglestone Ben, owned by Lorna, Countess Howe, won 19 challenge certificates in 1935-8.*

Above: *Lawnwoods Hot Chocolate, the author's own dog, is American and English Champion.*

two other Sh Ch Chocolate bitches and one Sh Ch Chocolate dog: full Champion Lawnwoods Hot Chocolate who went to America and became the only American and English Chocolate Labrador dog.

Sandylands Kennel
Any mention of Labradors must always include the name of Mrs Gwen Broadley and her Sandylands Kennel. Building on the foundation that Lorna, Countess Howe laid, Gwen built a wonderful reputation for breeding dogs of the highest merit and outstanding type and temperament, and her opinions are much sought after all over the world. The names of Ch Sandylands Tandy and Ch Sandylands Mark can be seen on nearly every pedigree of today.

The United States
As in England, Labradors were also being recognized in America for their dual-purpose ability. The American Kennel Club recognized them officially in 1917, and well-known English trainers who lived in America supervised the training for field trials of dogs brought over from England.

The Honourable Franklin Lord, a great friend of Lorna, Countess Howe, acquired many dogs from her. One of them, sired by Ch Ingleston Ben to Banchory Traco, was Boli of Blake. He became the first American Champion.

The Labrador Retriever Club Inc was founded in 1931 and in the same year their first field trial was held.

Up to this time, the Labradors seemed to be predominantly black, but then Yellows began to be noticed: and Mr Lambert's bitch Golden Chance of Franklin was the first Yellow to win Best of Breed at a show in 1957, followed by Bickerton Salmon Queen winning Best in Show in 1962.

Gradually, well-known prefixes came to the fore, and can be found in many of today's pedigrees. To name but a few, Mrs Joan Read's 'Chidley', Mrs Howe's 'Rupert', Mr Averil Harriman's 'Arden' and Mr & Mrs James Warwick's 'Lockerbie'.

Chapter Two

CHOOSING AND CARE

ACQUIRING A LABRADOR

Characteristics

If you are keen to acquire a Labrador, it is important to consider the particular characteristics of the breed, both in terms of temperament and physical attributes of the adult dog, before thinking about selecting an individual.

Mature Labradors are fairly large and weighty dogs, strong and nimble with long, powerful and ever-wagging tails.

Dogs grow to about 23in (56cm) at the withers, weighing about 70-75lb (32-34kg); bitches are about one inch (2.5cm) shorter and weigh 55-70lb (25-32kg).

Labradors are noted for being good-tempered and can be trusted with children. They particularly love other dogs and human company. Therefore, the Labrador owner must be prepared to provide adequate companionship if they are to get the best from their dog. They are intelligent and agile, making good working dogs with a keen sense of smell and ability to pick up things tenderly with their soft mouths, vital for gundog work.

Below: *The Labrador is well-known for its affectionate and trustworthy temperament.*

Bottom: *Labradors enjoy a long country walk and the chance of retrieving the odd stick.*

CHOOSING A PUPPY

Pet, working or show dog?

If you want a family dog, you may be lucky enough to be able to choose from a litter of five or six, and you will perhaps be attracted to the one that jumps up out of the pile and comes forward to you to be stroked. A puppy that hangs back, or runs into a corner, is not going to be an extrovert.

A puppy intended as a working dog should be the lively one, who misses nothing and wants to be out of the box first; the one that can be seen picking up the toys and retrieving, but who may not have the finest show points.

If you wish to show, it would be advisable to approach a well-known breeder, who has consistent success in the show ring at the highest level of showing. He or she has the experience of knowing how his or her puppies develop, and how much show potential any puppy in the litter might have — although no breeder can guarantee a winner.

Always try to see the puppy's parents and its close relatives — if they are not present, look at photographs. For working dogs, it would be preferable to see mother doing a little retrieving and tracking.

Whichever you choose, you are hoping to take home a companion for the next 12 to 15 years, so your original expenditure will be only a small percentage of your overall outlay for years to come. The quality of the puppy will dictate the price, and you must expect to pay considerably more for a potential show specimen.

Dog or bitch?

Many people opt for a bitch because they believe that they are quieter and more companionable. But they do come into season twice yearly, and have to be looked after very carefully at this time and kept away from

Below: *Young Labrador puppies are small, cuddly and very appealing, but remember they grow into big, heavy dogs.*

Above: *These three little puppies show the three main coat colours of their breed: black, yellow and chocolate or liver.*

other dogs. Or, if you decide on neutering, spaying a bitch is more expensive than neutering a dog. Some may feel that a bitch is a better investment, particularly if it has show potential, given that if it grows on satisfactorily and fulfils all the criteria, a litter could be bred off her.

A dog will grow to be larger and more robust, but as the years go by, settles down and becomes a very faithful companion. A well-fenced garden and plenty of companionship is the key to success here. It is only the dog that is alone and bored at home that finally seeks a way out of the garden, looking for companionship.

Older puppies
Puppies are usually sold at eight weeks old. But for various reasons, sometimes people prefer an older puppy — perhaps taking one at six months. Certainly by this age one can see more of what the puppy is going to be like as an adult, and certainly it will have many of its early problems behind it. Of course, it will

be more expensive because the breeder has had to pay for all its inoculations and specialized care for six months — and you miss out on all the fun of having a young puppy scampering around.

Colour and number
Labradors are available in three colours: black, yellow and chocolate. Choice of colour varies according to individual preference, and I always feel that it is the character of the dog that counts most.

Occasionally, people feel that they would like to take two puppies. Here, I do suggest that they have both of the same sex; mixed sexes can lead to difficulties! While it is obviously nice for puppies to have companionship, it does mean double food bills. and leads to dependency on each other — weighed against which, great companionship and outdoor activities are more fun!

Pedigree
Finally, when your choice is made, it is a good idea to look at your new puppy's pedigree and have it explained. Always remember, however, that a puppy with many champions or field trial champions in its ancestry may not necessarily prove to be a better companion.

FINDING A PUPPY

Before buying a puppy, it is a good idea to make a few enquiries about where to find nicely bred puppies that have been well looked after. To do this, it is important to find a breeder of high standard in Labradors who values her reputation. Whether you are considering the puppy solely as a companion, or perhaps you intend using it for some rough shooting, obedience or even field trials, it is essential to know something about its background.

A useful shop window is the local show world, and in particular a Championship Dog Show. Here you will find breeders willing to talk about their breed, and they will be able to recommend litters, if they have none of their own to offer. At this venue you can really see the breed and the three colours close up, and compare dogs with bitches. Visit field trials and working tests if your interests are in working dogs.

In the USA *Dog World,* published monthly, *Pure Bred Dogs* and *The American Kennel Gazette* have lists of good breeders. In Britain shows are advertised in national dog papers and the *Kennel Gazette,* which also publishes the names of the secretaries of many breed societies, who are only too willing to help and advise you in buying a puppy.

Below: *A healthy, well-bred puppy is alert with good bone, a shiny coat and bright eyes.*

Visiting a breeding establishment
Once you have decided on colour, sex and type of Labrador you wish to own, you should arrange to visit the breeder of your choice. Be sure to wear clean clothes and shoes, and do not expect to be allowed to handle puppies. Infections can easily be carried unknowingly from home to home.

I prefer to meet prospective puppy owners before the puppies are born. This gives the buyers the opportunity of ironing out any difficulties over puppy ownership that might be worrying them, and the breeder can decide whether she feels that her puppies are likely to be suitable for the buyer — or indeed if the buyer is suitable to have a puppy. General expenses and cost of feeding can be discussed, and the future environment for the puppy can be talked about. Finally, arrangements can be made for viewing the puppies when they are born, and for their eventual collection.

Note on your first visit if the outside runs and kennels are clean,

Above: *A good breeder of Labradors will have clean outside kennels and runs with happy, well-groomed dogs — an ideal place to purchase your Labrador puppy.*

with fresh bedding; that there is fresh water in bowls or buckets readily available, and the kennel occupants are happy, well-groomed and cheerful. Above all, state what your aims are, and you will find that the breeder of your selection will be only too happy to try to accommodate you.

I find that puppies born in the breeder's house, and kept there until their eyes open, and where they begin to hear household noises, are far more socialized by humans handling and cuddling them, than puppies that are kept outside in a kennel with their mother.

When making your final decision, make sure that the puppy's ears and teeth are clean, its eyes are clear and bright, its coat is clean and healthy and its nails short — and that it scampers around, full of fun.

BRINGING YOUR PUPPY HOME

Puppies are usually ready to go to
their new homes at between seven
and eight weeks, and certainly
socializing with humans should have
begun at six weeks.

The journey
If you are travelling far, it would be
wise for the puppy to miss its early
meal so that it will travel in comfort
and not feel sick. When you go to
collect it, be prepared with a
blanket, newspapers and towels —
and a damp cloth. When it is put
into your arms, support it under the
chest, rump and back legs, and
travel with it on your knee. Never
put it alone in the back of the car.

You will be given a copy of its
pedigree, Kennel Club registration
papers, a diet sheet with times of
feeding and correct quantities, a
note of the last date of worming,
some samples of food that it is used
to, and probably a certificate of

insurance for the first few weeks.
Later, this can be automatically
extended to a year's cover.

Preparation and equipment
You will need to decide where the
new puppy's accommodation will be
— in the kitchen, utility room or
boiler house would be suitable.

Bedding Wherever you choose, it
will need a bed. To begin with a
cardboard box free of staples, with a
blanket (in winter a warm radiator),
and a supply of newspapers on the
floor, that can be changed if
mishaps occur, is a must. Later on
the bedding can be replaced by a
stout purpose-made wooden box, or
a hard plastic dog basket.

Feeding bowls Your puppy will
need its own feeding dish and one

Below: *Bowls for food and water.
The steel variety in the background
is the best to use.*

25

for water — preferably made of steel, and untippable! A pottery bowl could end up being carried complete with contents, and tipped out on a precious carpet. A plastic dish could be lethal if bits of plastic are swallowed. Plastics cause obstructions in the digestive tract not visible on X-rays.

Wire pen If the puppy is to stay in the kitchen, a wire pen is very useful. Not only will it keep it from under your feet when you are handling hot things, but if its bed is placed within its bounds, it will learn very quickly that its own bed is where it must stay. There are proprietary puppy pens available, or use garden refuse containers.

Toys A few useful hard rubber bones and dumbells will serve adequately as preliminary toys, to be superseded later by a well-boiled middle section of a marrow bone.

Persuade the younger members of the family to keep their plastic toys and all their belongings in their bedrooms. This will save a lot of minor heartbreaks for children who might otherwise find their favourite toys partially demolished by the puppy when your back is turned. You have to remember that your Labrador was born and bred to retrieve, and this instinct will stay with it all its life. Carefully handled in the early stage, this can be channelled into an interesting relationship with the family later on.

Collapsible kennel If you intend the puppy to travel by car often this is a useful asset which will fit in the car, and where the puppy can be left.

Outdoor kennel and run Some people like to have an outdoor kennel, and even an attached run. This is a good idea in essence, so long as the dog is not left there on its own all day. These can be built by a handy-man or bought from well-known kennel makers. Bedding here could be either woodwool or a white synthetic sheepskin-like rug that resembles lambswool.

Only if the kennel is a minimum of

Above: *Wire pens may not look attractive, but they confine the young puppy to its own area while allowing it to see what is going on around it.*

Right: *Play with a toy or ball daily in the garden will provide the Labrador puppy with the right amount of exercise.*

Bottom right: *Once your Labrador has reached maturity, do not give in to the appealing looks for extra food or titbits.*

6ft (1.8m) high can a heat lamp be put in safely. Unless the weather is really freezing, an adult Labrador's thick, warm coat will cope with cold conditions.

EXERCISE FOR THE PUPPY

As a very young puppy, and up to six months of age, a Labrador requires very little exercise indeed. In fact, an occasional run around the garden is quite sufficient.

Once the inoculation period is over, a quiet local walk, not more than ¼ mile (0.4km), on a lead is more than adequate until the puppy is over six months of age.

More puppies are over-exercised than the opposite. A dog's bones do not really calcify until they are six months old or more, and a long arduous romp over fields before this time is like taking a toddler for a walk along a two-mile beach.

Naturally puppies want to please you, and be with you, and will over-tax themselves to the point of exhaustion before flopping down. Considerable damage can result, especially as Labradors, properly fed, will be quite round and roly-poly at this age, and it is vital that they stay plump if they are to develop into fine adults.

Meanwhile, play in the garden is adequate, provided that the garden is well fenced in upwards of 6ft (1.8m) from the ground. If this is organized before the puppy arrives, it will not even think about getting out of the garden — particularly as you intend to give it all the companionship it needs. (Some gardens have fish ponds, and provision must be made to fence off or cover them.

FEEDING

Proprietary dog foods

In the last few years great scientific strides have been made in the manufacture of dog and cat foods. For example, there is a great assortment of biscuit meal to choose from. Some include dehydrated meat; and a flake-type meal has been developed, consisting of a base of wheat, corn and maize, to which different manufacturers add dried vegetables and meat, thus making it into a complete maintenance feed.

Growing puppies are catered for, and special food, that includes calcium, phosphate and many trace elements suitable for their complete daily growth requirements, is easily obtainable.

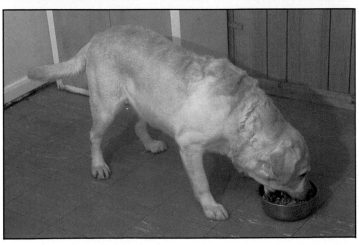

There is also an expanded nut-type dry dog food, which swells in the stomach. Fresh, frozen or canned meat, including tripe is available.

Although breeders usually suggest exact amounts of food for growth at certain ages, these amounts are calculated on the conditions at the breeder's home. If you only give the same quantity of food, and at the same time unwisely subject your puppy to a great deal more exercise than it is used to, its body and bone growth may suffer. At the end of 12 months, although the dog is maturing, it may look thinner than most, and may not have as much bone as he should. Once lost, good bone can never be regained.

Diet for puppies

Try to keep exactly to the diet and feeding times that your puppy was used to, at least for the first week. It must be quite disturbing for a puppy to change homes, especially leaving brothers and sisters and suddenly being on its own.

Once a puppy is established in its new routine at home, and a week or so has gone by, you may feel that you want to change its diet a little. The golden rule is to change only one meal at a time over the period of a few days, and watch and check

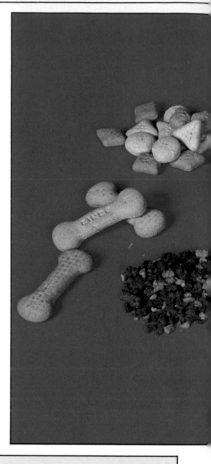

Suggested puppy diets

At 8 weeks; puppy weighing 12-16lb (5.5-7kg)

Breakfast:	6oz (200g) raw chicken mince or very lean minced beef
	1 handful puppy meal
	1 teaspoon calcium phosphate supplement
Midday:	As breakfast but without supplement **OR**
Late afternoon:	7oz (199g) canned rice pudding with equal water
Mid-evening:	As breakfast but without supplement

At 12 weeks; puppy weighing 20-24lb (9-11kg)

Breakfast:	8oz (250g) meat
	2 handfuls puppy meal
	1 teaspoon calcium phosphate supplement
Mid-morning:	As breakfast but without supplement **OR**
Early afternoon	7oz (199g) canned rice pudding with equal water
Evening:	As breakfast but without supplement

Always have fresh water available.

that it suits it. Whatever diet it is on the quantity, of course, will need to be increased as it grows. Although most breeders have different ideas about the sort of food they use when rearing puppies, the quantity different breeders recommend is usually similar.

I prefer not to use cow's milk at all. I do not consider it a natural food for dogs, so I feed an excellent product of raw chicken mince with puppy meal, and a calcium phosphate additive. I also give rice pudding, cheese, eggs, fish and goat's milk as welcome additions to the diet.

So at eight weeks of age, I would suggest following the diet chart opposite as a good regime for a puppy that weighed between 12 and 16 lb (5.5-7kg).

Above: *Various types of dog foods (clockwise from top right): fresh meat; canned dog food with mixer; semi-moist food; dry mixer; dry complete food; dog biscuits.*

Rate of growth
The Labrador grows quickly from eight to twelve weeks; not quite so much between three and six months; and growth levels out between six months and a year. Nevertheless, adequate food is essential for rapid growth, and the well-bred substantial puppy of a year is the result of months of good feeding up to that age.

The young adult dog
As a youngster, your dog will naturally go a little gangly — like a

29

human teenager — but as the months go by, and it slowly matures, it will grow into the characteristic sturdy Labrador.

By the time your puppy has reached the age of four months it should be eating three times a day. It could have either a meat and biscuit meal consisting of 12oz meat to 4oz (350:100g) biscuit morning and night with a cereal and milk or rice pudding meal at midday, or three meals a day of 8oz meat to 3oz (200:80g) biscuit plus calcium.

By six months the middle meal may be dropped, so that it is fed morning and evening.

By nine months you may prefer to feed once daily, but intake must be maintained at at least 1lb (450g) of meat a day with about 8oz (200g) of biscuit meal plus calcium.

Older dogs

As dogs grow less active later in life, their diets should be reduced accordingly. Labradors are known for their appealing, 'never-been-fed' look, and by six years of age are very adept at putting over their case well, to convince us that they are about to fade away from hunger! But, for their own good, keep them from becoming obese, because otherwise the layers of fat that have

accumulated will impair the function of the heart and lead to a shorter life-span.

PLAY AND REST

At home, right from the start, it is a good idea to give the puppy a set time to play once or twice a day with a human. This play can offset boredom, and can be educational for the young dog. Five minutes playing at searching for and retrieving a ball will come in useful later in life when serious training is to begin.

After play, the puppy will happily settle down to sleep for a couple of hours. This will form a longlasting habit where it knows it must retire to its own bed and not be a nuisance to the household. Sooner or later you will invite guests to your home who may not like dogs, or at best not want them continually interrupting the conversation.

Small pups need a great deal of rest, and I would suggest, if possible, an outhouse, made into a convenient kennel where it can sleep for a couple of hours morning and

---

Below: *Play with a Labrador puppy should take place in an enclosed, well-fenced area.*

afternoon. If this habit is formed as as puppy, later on it will always have a place of its own to go to, particularly after exercise over wet fields or such. There will be times in the future when you may not want your dog around, and if you have a place and routine established the puppy will not bark incessantly because it is being pushed out for a while.

INOCULATIONS

At approximately 12 weeks of age all puppies must be inoculated against Hepatitis, Leptospirosis, Canine Distemper and Canine Parvovirus.

Up until this time, the antibodies provided by their own dam have given them protection and would, in themselves, inhibit the vaccine from taking effect. These vaccinations are given in two injections administered two weeks apart. Not until your puppy has received its second dose is it safe to take it for walks in the street or to meet other dogs.

In countries where Rabies is established, the first Rabies vaccine should be given at approximately 12 weeks of age and a second injection at 14-16 weeks of age.

HOME HEALTH CARE

Upset stomach
Overfeeding, or giving food that is not yet suitable for a puppy's digestion, such as meat with too much fat on it, will give rise to vomiting, diarrhoea and refusal to eat. This is nature's way of telling the puppy to give its stomach a rest.

Left: *This small puppy takes its vital rest safely on the knees of its young owner.*

Below: *Two Labradors following their natural instincts — enjoying a game with a stick.*

The first thing to do is *starve* it of solids — never try giving milky or human invalid diets. Leave it without food for 24 hours, offering honey and water every two hours. If sickness stops after this time and there is no more diarrhoea, feel free to introduce about 4oz (100g) of well-minced boiled fish. Later in the day, if all is still well, try fish again with a tablespoon of boiled rice. If improvement continues, increase the amounts slowly the next day, and gradually return to normal diet, eliminating, of course, anything that you may feel has upset it. Perhaps it was given too big a ration of biscuit to meat — in which case there would be an excess of carbohydrate.

If it is still sick and has diarrhoea after the first 24 hours, it must be seen by a veterinarian. **Never try different foods** one after the other in an effort to make it eat.

If diarrhoea in the first instance is blood-stained and foul smelling, expert advice must be obtained without further delay! Puppies can so easily dehydrate quickly because of loss of fluids.

Quite often, the continued feeding of fatty meat can lead to a condition where the pancreas starts to malfunction. It seems to give up producing the enzymes vital to the puppy's digestive system. Symptomatically, the puppy will refuse food and its motions will be grey. Veterinarians will, of course, diagnose and treat the condition — but it is very debilitating to the puppy if it is allowed to continue.

Parasites

Roundworms Most puppies have these worms (Toxocara canis); they are born with the larvae in their bodies, which develop into adult worms by the time the puppy is two weeks of age. The adult worm can be up to 5in (13cm) long and produces microscopic eggs which can exist in the ground or in your home for a very long time. They are a health hazard, particularly to young children in warm, damp conditions.

You should make a note of the dates when the puppy was wormed

Above: *A light micrograph of the larval stage of Toxocara canis, or dog roundworm, which can cause illness in humans.*

when you collect it from the breeder. Ideally, it will have been wormed at two and a half to three weeks of age, and subsequently at two-week intervals. The worming treatment should continue every two weeks until the puppy reaches three months of age, then again at six months of age. Visit your veterinarian to discuss the worming programme and to obtain the necessary treatment — usually in tablet form. Proprietary preparations are only about 60% effective.

Adult Labradors should be treated once every six months throughout their lives.

Tapeworms Seek veterinary advice when you suspect tapeworms. They are not directly a health hazard to the family (with one rare exception

— see below) but proprietary remedies are rarely effective. The worm needs a secondary host, usually a rodent or flea, to complete its lifecycle. A sign of infection is the appearance of segments of the worm crawling around the dog's anus; they resemble cucumber seeds or grains of rice.

In areas where hydatid disease is present, regular tapeworm doses should be administered. This tapeworm of dogs is contracted from sheep or deer, and the eggs can infect people.

There are few signs of illness associated with tapeworms in dogs, except in heavy infestation when diarrhoea and weight loss occur.

Heartworms These are parasitic worms that are found in dogs' hearts. Dogs are the only mammals commonly affected, and the worm is transmitted by a mosquito. It is found in Africa, Asia and in large areas of the US, particularly the East Coast. In areas where the disease is endemic, daily preventative treatment is essential during the mosquito season. Seek local veterinary advice, and have yearly blood tests to confirm freedom from the infection.

Fleas These are very common, and they are not particular about where they live or who they bite. They have increased with the advent of central heating and fitted carpets. Fleas do not need to live on you or your pet; they just need a warm-blooded body to feed off when they are hungry. Because they are small and active, you may not actually see them. But you can spot where they have been by noticing the dark brown droppings when you are grooming.

Flea control is an important part of pet care. They can cause skin problems if your pet is allergic to their bite, and they can also cause you to have irritating red spots. Insecticides are now available which actually inhibit flea reproduction — a great advance. It is vital to treat your dog and its environment at the same time. When using insecticides,

follow the manufacturer's instructions carefully. These products must kill the fleas but not the host.

Lice (pediculosis) Lice are spread by direct contact or by contaminated brushes and combs. They accumulate under mats of hair around the ears, neck and body openings causing intense irritation. If you suspect infestation, bathe your dog using an insecticidal shampoo. Lice live and breed entirely on the dog, so it is not vital to treat the dog's environment as well.

Ticks Dogs can pick up ticks by running through grass, woods or sandy beaches. These blood-sucking insects bury their barbed mouths firmly into the dog's skin, causing irritation and often resulting in secondary skin infections. To remove adult ticks, soak them with ether, surgical spirit or tick spray. This will loosen the head and mouthparts to enable the removal of the whole insect with tweezers. The dog can be regularly bathed in a tick dip to prevent infestation, especially if it is in contact with sheep. The dog's environment should be vigorously disinfected as in some countries ticks transmit serious diseases such as anaplasmosis and babesiosis, and can cause tick paralysis.

Ear mites These mites live on skin debris on the surface of the ear canal. They can cause intense irritation and the production of reddish-brown crusts. The infection is highly contagious and is especially prevalent in young animals. Mineral oils combined with an insecticide are effective as long as the treatment is maintained for a four-week period. The dog's environment should be treated as thoroughly as the dog itself.

Cheyletiella mites (walking dandruff) This is a parasite that can cause unpleasant irritation to the owner as well as the pet host. The mites live only on the host and consequently are easier to deal with.

The mites and eggs can be seen with a magnifying lens, but the appearance of fine dandruff on the coat gives a clue to their presence. Most insecticides are effective but should be applied three times at weekly intervals.

Scabies (sarcoptic mange) This mite produces an intensely itchy, non-seasonal, transmissible infection. The mites burrow in the superficial layers of the skin, and can live on human beings for at least six days. The infection is highly contagious and young animals are more susceptible.

As the mite lives most of its life below the surface of the skin, it can be difficult to diagnose, even by repeated skin scrapings examined microscopically. Your veterinarian may make a diagnosis purely on the appearance of the patient. Although insecticides are effective, other medications will need to be used to relieve irritation and remove skin scale. Again, the dog's environment should be treated with an insecticide at the same time.

Demodectic mange This is a curious parasite which can exist in large numbers of dogs without causing symptoms. When it does, treatment can be lengthy and difficult. Most animals can now be cured, although because the illness

may represent an immune failure, dogs having had the disease should not be bred from, unless the condition was only transient. Seek expert veterinary advice.

Eyes
If the eyes are inflamed or discharging pus, check for foreign bodies such as grass seeds, then bathe using cotton wool and lukewarm water or an ordinary proprietary eye wash. You must, however, go ahead and seek veterinary advice immediately.

Ears
These should be examined regularly to make sure they are clean and sweet-smelling. If there is any dark brown discharge or unpleasant odour, or if your dog persistently shakes its head or scratches its ears, you will need prompt veterinary advice.

Clean the ears weekly by dusting the inside with medicated ear powder.

Teeth
Between 3½ and 4½ months, the puppy's baby or milk teeth start to

Below: *Let your veterinarian clean your dog's teeth periodically to remove the build-up of tartar.*

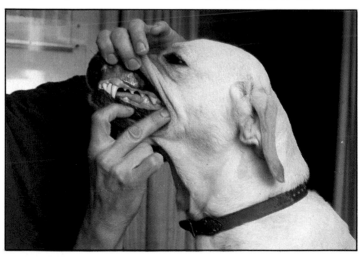

drop out and its permanent teeth begin to appear, 20 in the upper jaw and 22 in the lower jaw. While the puppy is teething, check the mouth frequently to see if the permanent teeth are pushing through the gums properly. Consult your veterinarian if problems develop, especially 'double' teeth (baby and permanent teeth in the same location) or overgrown or misplaced adult teeth.

The puppy may experience a little discomfort when teething, and a marrow bone will give the dog something to bite on to help it massage its gums.

Dog's teeth can accumulate tartar on the surface which needs to be removed. It is advisable to let your veterinarian periodically remove the

Above: *A good marrow bone is not only a source of calcium and an excellent object for your teething puppy to bite on; it is also pure heaven!*

tartar and polish the teeth. See also Chapter Three on dental problems.

If your Labrador is patient and willing, you can brush the teeth with a soft toothbrush and canine toothpaste once a week. It is best to introduce your dog to this operation early in life. If your dog is highly intolerant to teeth brushing, try an application of hydrogen peroxide mouthwash or baking salt dissolved in water applied with a soft rag wrapped around your finger.

Nails

These may grow long and claw-like while a puppy is indoors. Trim them carefully a little at a time using nail clippers — the guillotine type are probably the best to use. Great care must be taken not to cut the soft, fleshy area inside the nail called the quick, which contains the nerves and blood supply. If you look closely at the nail, particularly if it is light in colour, the quick will show up clearly as a pink vein. If you do cause the nail to bleed, apply a nail blood-clotting solution commercially available to stop the blood flow. Once your Labrador can go outside, normal exercise on hard surfaces should keep the nails short. But it is nevertheless advisable to check them monthly to see if they need trimming.

Grooming

Grooming daily is a very good habit. You will require a steel comb with ½in (15mm) long teeth and a stiff bristle brush or a handglove. Brush the coat vigorously and then comb through to remove any dead hair.

A Labrador's coat is easy to keep clean — a quick rub down with a

Above: *Take great care when clipping your Labrador's claws not to damage the quick.*

towel or chamois leather when it comes in on a wet day, and a daily comb and brush is something it will soon learn to look forward to. Its coat is very weather-resistant due to the thick undercoat that keeps it warm, and the top coat is of such a texture that any mud or dirt will fall off within a couple of hours. Brushing helps to keep the skin in good condition, promoting good hair growth.

PUBLIC CONTROL

By law in England all dogs must have a collar with means of identification attached with its owner's name and address. Your dog should never be allowed out on its own — if it should cause an accident or damage in any way you, as its owner, are liable to pay for the damages.

The laws in England are often read to the letter by farmers to protect their sheep, and by game wardens to protect their deer, and not everybody who walks over country areas wants a big, bouncy strong dog jumping up at them — and of course, excess freedom up to the age of seven to eight months may cause irreparable damage to a puppy's young bone growth. In the USA the laws on dog control are very strict. Do not be tempted to let your dog loose in parks and country areas until you are quite sure it will come back to you on recall.

CAR TRAVEL

The earlier your dog begins to travel by car the less likelihood there is of motion sickness. Labradors love travelling, and view the car as their kennel-on-wheels. Always carry a bowl and water with you, and always remember to leave windows slightly open. Never leave a dog in an airless car on a hot day. One would only have to imagine being locked up in a greenhouse on a sunny day when the temperature climbs. Remember, even if you leave the car parked in the shade, it does not take long for the sun to move around, and often cloudy conditions can rapidly change to brilliant sunshine.

Dog guards are useful too in estate cars or station wagons as a means of restricting the dog to the back of the vehicle — but for a Labrador, it has to be a very strong one, or it will treat it with contempt!

Always have a lead with you in the car. You could have a puncture and need to get at a spare wheel directly under where the dog is sitting.

Below: *A basic grooming kit (from top, left to right): chamois leather; bristle brush; wide/medium tooth comb; guillotine nail clipper; hound glove.*

Above: *A dog must not annoy other people or their dogs. If it cannot learn to come to you as soon as it is called, keep it on a lead when out for a walk.*

Below: *Dogs should be taught to sit or lie quietly when travelling. They generally like the feeling of security which a cage or box such as the one shown here will provide.*

CARE OF OLDER LABRADORS

Many years have passed, and through thick and thin your dog has been a constant companion to you. Until now it has been a creature of habit: obedient, clean and always ready and willing to go out for walks and be with the family.

Gradually you notice a slowing down. Perhaps it takes more time to get up in the morning, lies around more and does not come so quickly and easily when you call, except when there is food in the offing! It may have difficulty in keeping up with you on a brisk walk and maybe its legs are not quite so well co-ordinated. It might lose a little confidence, and need help to get in and out of cars, and may eat its meals more slowly, so they may need to be divided into two or three portions daily.

It may prefer to rest on furniture during the day, because it is away from draughts. It may become arthritic, and suffer decaying teeth, partial blindness from senile cataracts, liver and kidney malfunctions, or in the case of a bitch, possible uterine problems, and could develop a few lumps and bumps in various parts of its body.

I suggest that it is checked over by your veterinarian, twice yearly, so that it can be given palliative treatments for any conditions that might have arisen during the preceding few months.

Perhaps you are beginning to wonder how long this stoic old companion of yours can manage to put up with its new ailments so cheerfully, and when you should start to think about preserving its dignity.

Provided that it seems to be reasonably free from pain, distress and discomfort, can walk and balance reasonably well, be quite aware of its immediate surroundings, able to eat and drink without too much difficulty, and is keeping to its usual weight, has no visible cysts and tumours, and is not incontinent, it can humanely stay with you a little longer.

Everybody finds it extremely hard to make a final decision about euthanasia for their dogs, and I can only say that once the decision has been taken, and only then, can you look back and know that your resolution to relieve your old friend's suffering was right. We should not be haunted by the memory of pain and distress; we should be able to remember only the joy our dogs gave us during their lifetime.

Below: *A gentle amble along a seashore or over a field will keep older dogs happy.*

Chapter Three

BASIC TRAINING

Toilet training
Elementary obedience
Obedience away from home
Obedience classes

41

Labrador puppies are very curious and mischievous by nature, and once yours has settled down with you in its new environment, it will be busy exploring everywhere in the house.

Try to discourage it from getting onto furniture and climbing stairs. Besides being out of sight if it goes to explore, it could also damage its bones running up and down the stairs. From the beginning try to teach it where it may and may not go; where its bed is, and where it is to go to its toilet in the garden or an appropriate, enclosed area outside.

TOILET TRAINING

Once established in its new home, the puppy will begin to show its character — and will be all too willing to please you. Toilet training must begin immediately. Pick it up every time it wakes, or has eaten, take it outside and stand with it while it performs; following this up with a word of praise, and take it back indoors again. As it grows up, it will not need to go out so often.

Within two weeks it should be standing at the door, asking to go out. Never scold if it makes a mistake. Bitches are easier to train

Below: *A young Labrador must obey commands to sit and stay. Try practising in the house.*

Bottom: *Always use the same commands, especially in toilet training, to avoid confusing your puppy.*

than dogs, because they like to keep to one spot — but from the beginning for either dog or bitch, make sure it does not perform on the grass in full view — or in no time you will have brown patches on the formerly green grass.

Your puppy will soon get into the routine of going outside to relieve itself directly after eating and immediately after waking from a long sleep. At other times the observant owner will see it looking around for a place to go, and can instantly take it outside. It is most important to give full praise at every performance!

ELEMENTARY OBEDIENCE

The Labrador is a breed of dog that is only too willing to please, so your puppy will naturally learn the first commands of obedience like 'sit', 'stay' and 'come', easily. Encourage it to sit and stay on command, and give plenty of praise so that it understands that it has behaved correctly. Always call your puppy by its name and always make a fuss of it when it does what is asked of it.

All training should be made happy and fun for a puppy; scolding only makes it unhappy and unlikely to understand what wrong it has done — use a firm voice to say 'no', and it will understand by the tone of voice.

If you are having an 'off' day, forget about training for that day, because you may do more harm than good! Likewise, do not overtrain, or you will only end up confusing your dog. If problems arise, go back to square one and start all over again.

A trained dog will be happier, will look forward to being constantly with you as a well-behaved member of the family, and you will be able to do many enjoyable things together.

There are many books written on obedience, and many on training the working dog, all of which are well worth reading (see appendix for full details of recommended further reading).

Below: *A Labrador always wants to please, so don't forget to praise him, especially after a reprimand, to restore confidence.*

Collar and lead

To get the puppy used to its collar and lead, leave the lead on for a few minutes and let it walk about with it trailing. It is quite likely that it will pick it up and carry it in its mouth. If it does this, you can carry the handle and walk forward — and this leads naturally to furthering its training.

Once it has finished its inoculations, your puppy can begin a very small amount of road walking, getting it used to traffic and other noises. It must learn to go to the toilet in the gutter, and it is advisable to carry some means of disposal should an accident happen. It is preferable to train a dog to urinate in your own garden, rather than in any public place, and many cities have bye-laws concerning dogs fouling pavements and play areas, and quite rightly too!

'Sit', 'heel' and 'stay'

As your puppy grows up, further training in the garden, with a rope lead checking it as it pulls, is a must. First, sit it and then begin walking, telling it to 'heel'. With its head coming no further forward than your knee, sit the dog again and pat and praise it so that it knows it has behaved correctly. For a few minutes, continue up the path with sit and heel, followed by sit and praise, constantly letting it know it is pleasing you.

Below: *A 'poop-scoop' for use on any occasion to remove excrement quickly and hygienically.*

Bottom left: *A young Labrador learning to sit and wait for the command 'heel' before walking forward on a check lead.*

Bottom right: *This illustrates your aim in training — the dog is walking to heel without pulling forward on the lead.*

Once it has got the idea, the sit can be turned into a sit and stay. Sit the dog and turn to face it with the palm of your right hand raised towards it. Keep repeating 'stay' and then pat and praise it.

The next step is to sit and stay the dog while you back off one step. Repeat the word 'stay', then return and make a big fuss of it. Progress by backing one step only at a time, and always return before it moves towards you. If it does move, go right back and sit it exactly where you started, and start again at square one. Do not overdo the exercise — 5 minutes daily is quite enough — and always end on a good note with lots of praise and a titbit as a reward. This way, it can be made to appear like a game to your dog.

After a while, during stays, gently take the lead off from time to time, and as its sits and stays improve, along with its heel work, you will be able to start working without a lead.

Recall
Start to walk the puppy to heel around the garden, and sit it at a

Above: *Teaching the Labrador to sit. Always precede every command with the dog's name: 'Toby, sit'.*

distance, and start the recall. You need to walk away backwards, saying continuously, 'stay' until you are some way from the dog. Then standing upright, either clap your hands on your legs, or clap hands and call its name and 'come!'

Getting your dog to come directly to you right from the start, perhaps bribing with a reward, is probably the most important exercise you can teach, because instant obedience in returning is essential when you are out. A dog must be made to feel extremely happy to return to you without even thinking about other distractions. So, again, profuse praise is valuable. If it plays about, sit down with your back to it and eventually it will return. Better in the garden, than in open countryside!

'Down'
Labradors are naturally exuberant and tend to jump up if given the chance. Right from eight weeks of

45

age, only fuss a dog in a sitting position. Push it down gently if it jumps up as a greeting, and later be ready with your knee to help you push it back into the sit position.

If the habit has got out of control, put a rope lead on the puppy, and as it rushes forward to greet you, get a helper to pull back hard on the lead, shouting 'no', 'down'. Very quickly, the dog will realize what an uncomfortable exercise that was.

Below: *You can progress to 'sit-stay' off the lead once you have practised it on the lead.*

Centre: *Practising the recall. As you and your dog progress, it will learn to have more confidence in you.*

Bottom: *Your Labrador should be taught to lie down and stay when told. If its concentration wanes, end the training session.*

OBEDIENCE AWAY FROM HOME

Assuming that you have diligently followed my suggestions, your dog should be reasonably biddable by the time you take it out into the wide open spaces. Over the first months of your relationship you should have developed an intelligent rapport with each other and, as the dog's natural instincts dictate, it wants only to

Below: *A check chain is placed around the dog's neck with ring at lowest point of gravity. Only use in obedience training.*

Bottom: *From top — show-type slip leads, canvas and leather; long lead and check chain for use at obedience classes; stout leather collar and lead; long chain lead; check chain ready to put on; owner's whistle.*

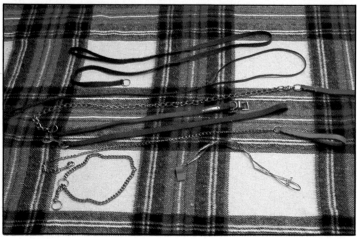

please you. It will enjoy its longer walks and will hopefully obey all your commands.

Constant revision of early schooling is, of course, needed right from the beginning, to help a puppy get used to extra freedom. Obviously there will be many distractions, and it is up to you as its teacher to anticipate difficulties before they actually arise. So, to begin with it should remain on a lead under your complete control until you feel that you can trust it in the various situations that arise.

I find that using a whistle and calling the dog back with two short blasts, always giving a biscuit when it returns, creates a really good habit and keeps its attention.

At six months your puppy should have learnt to sit and stay on command, or to come when called, despite distractions. Continue these lessons daily in the garden. Encourage it to stay a little longer every day, and to learn to retrieve and bring a ball or dummy back to you (see below), and sit beside you — always praising well and always finishing the lesson on a good note. Until you have perfected sit, stay and recall at home, it would be wise not to let your puppy off the lead in public parks, etc.

If you always keep the lessons short, with simple commands, plenty of praise and very slowly increasing the length daily, the greater the bond is formed between you, and you will end up with a grown dog to be very proud of.

Retrieving
By now your sit and stay commands can also be used for elementary retrieving. Make the dog sit and stay when you throw a ball, and encourage it to bring it back to you. If it does not, turn and run away and when it eventually catches up with you, take the ball and praise the dog. Soon it will learn that if it does what you want you will throw the ball again! Later you can improve on this exercise by hiding the ball and sending the dog out to search for it — saying 'get on', 'find' or 'seek'.

In the car
Obedience is vital in a dog travelling by car. In the car, and particularly if you have an estate car (or station wagon), it must learn to sit quietly while travelling, in the part of the

---

Below left: *A preliminary lesson in retrieving. The dog must be taught to sit and stay whilst the dummy (buffer) is thrown.*

Below: *The dog must learn to retrieve the dummy and bring it back to hand and keep it in its mouth until the owner takes it.*

vehicle appointed for it. It must also learn to sit and stay while car doors and/or tail-gates are being opened, and must always be made to sit and wait before being allowed to jump down out of the car. Of course, when very small, help will be needed for it to get both in and out of the car.

All this can be practised in the confines of your garden before the Labrador is six months old, as a preliminary measure.

OBEDIENCE CLASSES

In many places obedience classes are run weekly, where experienced trainers are on hand to advise the pupils. Dogs benefit greatly from these sessions, which are normally run over a twelve-week period, and at them you will meet other owners and problems are discussed. At the same time your dog will learn to accept the company of other dogs of various breeds.

The basic lessons of heel work, sit, stay, and recall are not only made more exact, but additional lessons such as retrieving, scent discrimination, 'sent away' and other commands will add to the repertoire of your dog. Labradors can do quite well in general obedience tests, though they usually show much greater enthusiasm for gundog working tests (see Chapter Six on gundogs, and Chapter Seven on working tests), but the simple training classes will be a further step down the road to improved obedience.

Left: *Young puppies and old dogs must always be helped to get in and out of vehicles.*

Below: *It is equally important that owners are correctly trained in handling their dogs.*

Chapter Four

VETERINARY CARE

Visiting your veterinarian
Infections prevented by vaccination
A-Z of veterinary problems
Inherited defects
Emergencies

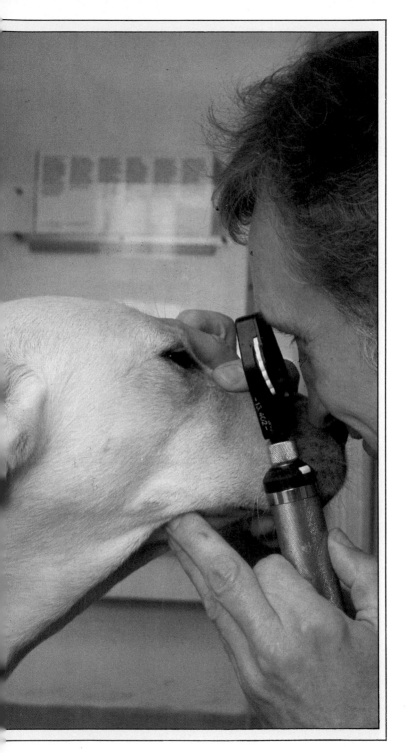

51

VISITING YOUR VETERINARIAN

It is important to find a sympathetic veterinarian to look after your Labrador, and to make sure you know how and when to contact him or her in an emergency. A veterinarian may even be able to advise you on where to purchase a sound Labrador, free from any inherited defects that can occur in the breed, such as PRA (Progressive Retinal Atrophy) and HD (Hip Dysplasia).

Examining the puppy

Now for your puppy's first examination. The veterinarian will be having a good look at the puppy while listening to your account of feeding habits, behaviour and how it is settling into the family. You should have the papers from the breeder with information on diet, worming and previous vaccinations. The veterinarian may ask for a stool sample to check for worms.

The temperature of the puppy will be taken — and ears, eyes, heart and joints checked. If the veterinarian suspects the presence of a serious congenital or hereditary defect, it may be advisable to send the puppy back to the breeder, particularly if you have plans to show or breed from your dog.

A health programme

Having passed the physical examination you must now discuss feeding and general management and a worming and vaccination programme.

If it is your first experience with a pet, make sure you have a list of questions ready, to cover all your queries.

INFECTIONS PREVENTED BY VACCINATION

Rabies

This is a virus disease that is always fatal once symptoms show. It can be transmitted to man. Rabies is a disease of the central nervous system, and manifests itself in two forms, 'furious' and 'dumb'. 'Furious' rabies is comparatively easy to diagnose. The 'dumb' form, which is characterised by paralysis, is not spectacular and is difficult to diagnose, despite being more common than the furious form.

Wildlife act as a reservoir for the disease: racoons and skunks in the US, vampire bats in South America, the mongoose in South Africa and the fox in Western and Eastern Europe.

Below: *Take you new puppy to the veterinarian for a health check soon after acquiring it.*

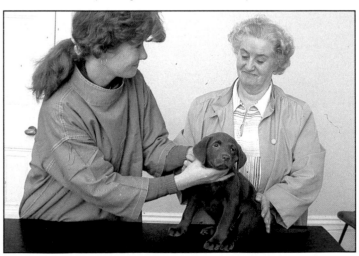

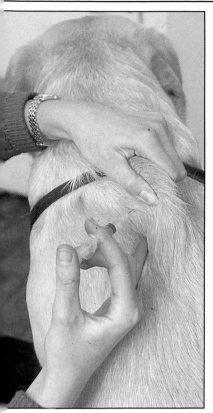

Above: *A vaccination against the common diseases — Hepatitis, leptospirosis, Canine Distemper, Canine Parvovirus — is combined and administered at about 10 and 12 weeks with annual boosters.*

Incubation can be between five days and ten months. Affected animals show a change in temperament, becoming highly restless and irritable. As the disease progresses there is weakness of the tail and legs, difficulty in swallowing, and drooping of the jaw and eyelids. The animal usually dies in a state of coma, following convulsive seizures in the furious form and paralysis in the dumb form.

Vaccination is now effective and is mandatory in some areas of the world, such as the USA. Booster vaccinations are yearly or biannually in some states.

Canine parvovirus (CPV)

A virulent disease of dogs only, but transmissible via clothing and footwear. The virus is resistant to most disinfectants and can remain alive up to a year in a house or kennel.

The disease causes depression, severe and prolonged vomiting, abdominal pain, and profuse diarrhoea with blood. Urgent vigorous, intensive treatment is necessary for several days, and the illness is often fatal.

Vaccination with live attenuated CPV is effective, and a yearly booster recommended.

Distemper

This is a virus disease transmitted from dog to dog, still common in dog pounds. Initially it presents like a cold — runny eyes, a cough, poor appetite and diarrhoea, followed some weeks later by nervous signs, muscle twitching, fits and paralysis. It may be accompanied by hyperkeratosis of the pads (hard pad).

This disease is often fatal but dedicated nursing can bring success. Your puppy should be vaccinated at 10 and 12 weeks and receive an annual booster.

Canine adenovirus infections

(a) Infectious hepatitis (canine adenovirus type, 1 CAV-1) This is another highly infectious viral disease, associated with nephritis (inflammation of the kidneys), eye disease, and liver damage. Infection is contracted from faeces and urine (recovered dogs may excrete the virus for six months). Puppies in their first year of life are most commonly affected, but dogs of any age are susceptible. Severely affected dogs die in as little as six to eight days. Blue eyes may be seen in the recovery stage.

There is also a respiratory form of this disease which is not so serious. (b) Canine adenovirus type 2 (CAV-2) This virus is implicated in some cases of contagious respiratory disease.

Vaccination against both illnesses is achieved by giving modified CAV 2 virus, and is boosted yearly.

Leptospirosis
(a) The liver form (Leptospirosis icterohaemorrhagiae)
A bacterial disease of dogs that can be passed to people, transmitted by rats and rat urine. The disease is characterised by sudden onset of fever, jaundice and severe depression. There may also be thirst, vomiting and bloody diarrhoea. Death may occur in two to three hours, but antibiotics given early and supportive treatment can be successful. Vaccination is effective and a yearly booster should be given.
(b) The kidney form (Leptospirosis canicola)
A similar bacterial disease, again infectious to man. This illness is transmitted via urine, and hence its name 'lamp-post disease'. Vomiting, depression and inflammation of the mouth with abdominal pain are the main symptoms. Antibiotics and supportive treatment are effective and vaccination with yearly boosters protective.

Kennel cough (infectious rhinotracheitis)
This is a condition caused by a cocktail of viruses and bacteria. Total protection against the disease may not yet be possible, but vaccines are available which give some protection. These are

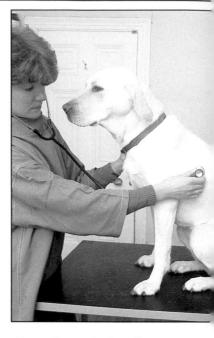

Above: *The veterinarian will use a stethoscope to check the heart and lungs for any signs of heart or respiratory problems.*

Below: *The veterinarian examines teeth and gums as part of a routine procedure, but Labradors on the whole have healthy teeth.*

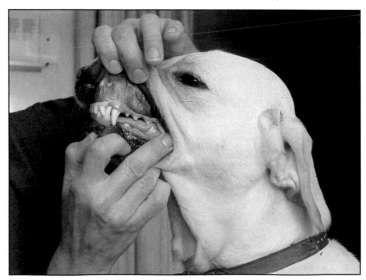

advisable before showing or kennelling. Their effectiveness may only last for six months.

A-Z OF VETERINARY PROBLEMS

Abscesses
These are paintful, pus-filled swellings, at the site of wounds or bites. They may occur in the anal glands, located each side of the anus (see anal problems below), in a tooth root or between the toes as the result of a lodged foreign body. In the first two cases, bathe with epsom salts and hot water until the abscess drains. You may need professional veterinary help if the infection spreads or if the abscess will not drain.

Anal problems
Biting around the root of the tail may indicate that the two small scent glands are blocked. Your veterinarian will be able to empty the glands. Fleas will attack the anal area, so look out for them (see page 33 on treatment of fleas). Worms also cause anal irritation (see page 32 on treatment of roundworms — *toxocara canis*).

Arthritis
This is usually osteoarthritis in the Labrador, and can be a crippling condition. It may occur as the result of either 1) an athletic injury and can be corrected surgically by repair of a torn ligament (commonly one of the cruciate ligaments in the stifle or knee), or 2) secondary to a joint disease (Hip Dysplasia or Osteochondritis). Spinal arthritis or spondylosis and disc disease are not uncommon in Labradors. Aspirin may be very effective but get an accurate diagnosis from your veterinarian and join a weight-watchers class for dogs. The less weight your dog carries, the less wear and tear there will be on the joints.

Bites and wounds
Always cleanse and clip the surrounding hair away. Puncture wounds often result in abscesses (see above).

Bronchitis
Coughing not caused by infectious diseases (see infections prevented by vaccination, page 54), may be bronchitis. This is an ailment not uncommon in the Labrador brought on by changes in the chest due to ageing and can be treated with drugs and correct diet.

Some older Labradors breathe noisily — associated with post-exercise tolerance, a muted bark and occasional collapse. This is caused by paralysis of the vocal cords due to a nerve injury and in most cases can be corrected surgically.

Colic
This is a result of over eating or scavenging. If gripe water does not help, consult your veterinarian. Severe distension of the stomach soon after eating is bloat, and this condition constitutes a *real* emergency.

Cut feet
These often bleed profusely. Apply a firm bandage to stop the blood flow. If the pad has been cut, it may not need stitching and, if there is no glass in the wound, it will heal within about 10 days. During this period, keep the would clean and bandaged. Be careful not to wet the bandage and remember to change it regularly.

Dental problems
Labradors generally have good teeth because they enjoy chewing things. This reduces the need for dental scaling but other problems arise due to over enthusiasm — worn crowns and split teeth caused by sticks, balls, stones or bones. Fortunately, veterinary dental care is now able to deal with these potentially painful problems, with root fillings, etc.

Diarrhoea
This can occur for a variety of reasons. Starve your Labrador for at least 24 hours and give small, frequent amounts of fluid. Then feed a bland diet of boiled white meat or eggs. Should the diarrhoea persist or blood is detected, visit your veterinarian without delay, taking with you a faecal sample.

55

Ear problems

The most common cause of head shaking in Labradors is ear mites (see page 33) but the sudden onset of shaking may be due to a grass awn or hay seed in the ear canal.

Swelling of the ear flap (aural haematoma) is a blood blister due to self inflicted damage to the blood vessels of the ear, caused by head shaking, rubbing or scratching. The cause of the inflammation needs treatment as well as the resulting haematoma, or the ear may end up a crinkled mess.

Eye conditions

All hunting dogs are prone to traumatic eye injury. Foreign bodies, such as grass awns and thorns, need to be removed under anaesthetic (sometimes just local) as soon as possible.

Corneal scratches need careful veterinary management; they are painful, the eye often being closed aggravated by the dog rubbing it, and the membrane around the eye swollen. Seek veterinary help.

Fits

These are alarming to witness and are usually epileptic (see epilepsy under inherited defects, page 58), but can occur for a variety of reasons such as poisoning and liver disease. They usually last a short time and are accompanied by frothing at the mouth, passing stools and urine. The dog may be dazed and unable to see or hear for a while. It may also be frighteneed and snap. Leave the dog alone in a quiet place, away from any stimulation from people or other animals. Remove anything in its vicinity that could be knocked over.

Kidney problems

These are more common in old age, often heralded by an increase in thirst. Water should always be available, but try and monitor the amount drunk by filling the bowl with a known amount of water (you can use a pint/litre milk bottle or carton). Take a urine sample when you visit your veterinarian, ideally in a sterile container.

Obesity

Obesity is the most common nutritional disease of pets caused by excess fatty tissue. It is more common in advancing age and in females.

Obesity will reduce an animal's enjoyment of life and its owners appreciation of it. More specifically:
1   It predisposes the animal to heart and liver disease
2   Increases the incidence of diabetes
3   Exacerbates arthritis and skin disease
4   Increases surgical risk
Overfeeding of puppies predisposes them to obesity for life, because fat cells grow larger. A strict feeding regime is essential. Keep a regular check.

If your pet has an obesity problem, do not feed anything more than the amount of food prescribed by your veterinarian. Engage the support of the whole family — no-one must give it extra tit-bits. Specific prescription diets are now available to save preparing complicated meals.

Heatstroke

This is most likely to occur in hot or sultry weather, usually in poorly ventilated cars. Cool the dog down by immersing it in cold water. Veterinary help is required if the dog is panting excessively or loosing consciousness.

Skin disease

Apart from parasitic and fungal diseases (see pages 32-33), the commonest skin problem in Labradors is wet eczema or 'hot spot'. This is a moist area of skin which appears very uncomfortable to the dog. It is an acute allergic response in the top layer of the skin and may respond to simple saline bathing and the application of astringents. It is important to find the cause of the trouble as well as ease the discomfort, so seek veterinary help without delay. However, accurate diagnosis may be difficult. Do not bath your dog before visiting the vet — you will remove the vital evidence!

Tumours

Early diagnosis of tumours may lead to a cure, so if you are worried about a lump, take veterinary advice early. Many tumours are benign, but do not be misled by the fact that a swelling does not hurt — tumours rarely do.

Vomiting

Dogs vomit readily and this is a protective mechanism — Labradors especially very often scavenge and eat rubbish.

Travel sickness is not uncommon, but will often be cured by increased familiarity with travelling.

Do not let the dog drink too much

water but provide little and often. A useful first aid is a white of an egg beaten up with half a cup of water and a teaspoon of sugar.

If the vomiting persists, or if blood is present in the vomit, seek urgent veterinary help.

INHERITED DEFECTS

Some inheritable defects of the Labrador should be avoidable by careful choice of puppies.

Osteo chondritis desiccais

This is not infrequently seen in the Labrador, usually in the elbow and shoulder joint but occasionally in the stifle and hock. This condition is seen between four and ten months and *may* have an inheritable basis. It is usually seen in well-nourished dogs growing rapidly and engaged in violent activity.

Below: *The veterinarian examines deep into the Labrador's ears for any signs of infection using an instrument called an auriscope.*

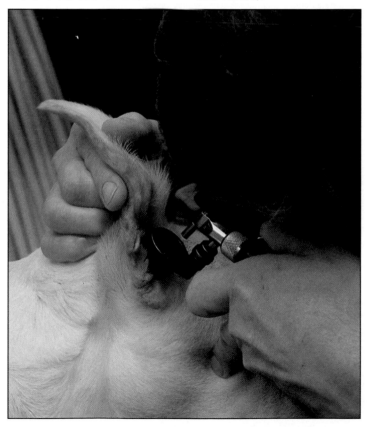

Epilepsy

This is well recognised in Labradors and may have an inheritable basis (see fits, page 56).

Primary Hereditary Cataract (HC)

This condition is recognised in the Labrador Retriever. Cataracts can be present in one or both eyes and these can lead to partial or total blindness.

Entropion

This is common in the Labrador. This turning in of the eyelid will cause the dog some pain and requires surgical correction. It may be avoided by careful selection of breeding stock.

Progressive Retinal Atropy (PRA)

PRA manifests itself as the central form, and is controlled by a

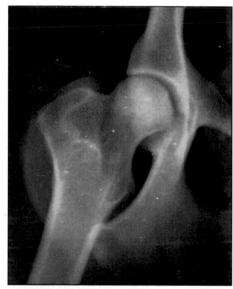

Normal hip

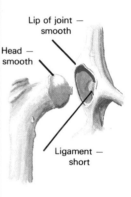

Lip of joint — smooth

Head — smooth

Ligament — short

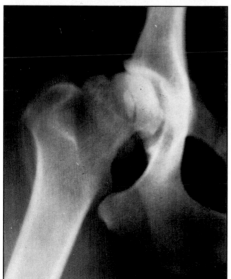

Hip with severe dysplasia

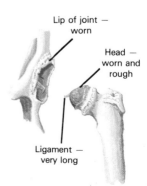

Lip of joint — worn

Head — worn and rough

Ligament — very long

dominant gene. It can be recognised early by a electroretinogram (advisable before breeding). It is a condition occasionally recognised in the Labrador.

Hip dysplasia

This is a malformation of the ball and socket joint of the hip. All authorities agree that this is an inheritable condition, but, sadly, the scheme to reduce its incidence is not foolproof because no one inheritable factor is concerned. In control schemes, X-rays are done under general anaesthetic at one year. Under the hip scoring scheme, each hip is scored from 0 to 53; the lower the score, the *less* the degree of hip dysplasia.

In the United States, a control scheme is run by the Orthopedic Foundation for Animals (OFA). The organisation checks dog's X-rays and pronounces them either afflicted or not afflicted; in the latter case, the dog is given an OFA registration number.

What is important to understand about the condition is that the dysplastic dog may be asymptomatic or show pronounced lameness.

Symptoms of lameness may show from four weeks of age, but are

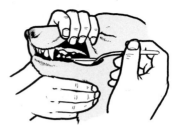

Above: *If you suspect that your dog has eaten a poisonous substance which is not corrosive, you can induce vomiting by administering a solution of salt or soda as shown.*

most apparent between 7 and 11 months and worse after prolonged or heavy exercise. There may be difficulty in rising, reluctance to move or play, aggressive behaviour due to pain, a wobbly swaying gait and poorly developed muscles of the rump and hind legs.

Many dogs are destroyed young with these symptoms, but with correct management and sometimes surgery, dogs with severe dysplasia can live useful, happy and pain-free lives.

EMERGENCIES

Normal hip

In this case, as shown in the illustration and X-ray above left, there is a perfectly smooth fit between the top of the thigh bone and the pelvis, like a ball and socket, and the ligament is short.

Hip with severe dysplasia

The ball and socket joint is malformed. Sometimes the cup or **acetabulum** *is too shallow, or the ball (femoral head) will be worn and misshapen with an elongated ligament. Some surgical procedures can help. The femoral head can be removed or, in some cases, the pectinious muscle can be cut, which causes the joint to pull apart, alleviating some pain. However, this method is not 100 per cent effective.*

Poisoning

With thousands of potentially poisonous substances in the environment, the following basic instructions should be followed:

1. If a poisonous substance is eaten, induce vomiting (1 teaspoon of hydrogen peroxide, salt or a lump of washing soda placed in the mouth) and save the vomit.
2. If the dog is in contact with toxic or corrosive material, wash the contaminated skin with large quantities of water.
3. If the dog becomes excited or has convulsions, try to protect the animal from injuring itself.
4. Bring the sample of suspected poison to the veterinarian with the dog. It is very useful to have some idea of the quantity eaten, if it was in tablet form.

Choking

This is manifested by the dog frantically tearing at its mouth. If a small ball is wedged at the back of the throat, remove it immediately as it will probably obstruct its airway.

Labradors chasing sticks can run onto a stick and tear the backs of their mouths. In this case, they may need hospital treatment.

A bone wedged across the roof of the mouth may sometimes be removed at home with a pair of pincers or tweezers.

Misalliance

If mismating occurs, abortion can be induced within 72 hours with oestrogens. This will prevent the eggs implanting and continmue the heat for a further three weeks. The

Above: *Regular health cnecks are strongly recommended to maintain your Labrador in good condition. These can be combined with your annual visits to the vet for vaccination boosters.*

hormone, unfortunately, can also cause endometritis and pyometritis requiring hysterectomy. Watch for signs of illness after the hormone injection, especially an increase in thirst or a pussy vaginal discharge.

Heart attack

Dogs do not suffer from heart attacks in the same way as humans, and heart conditions are usually treatable. Poor exercise tolerance and a cough related to exercise and excitement may suggest heart disease.

Stings and snake bites
Sudden acute pain and licking at a specific site should alert you to the possibility of a sting or snake bite. Snake bites to the throat are often fatal before you can get expert help, but bites further away from the head respond to nursing and steroids. Anti-snake venom is not always the best treatment.

Road accident
Do not panic and do not get bitten. Make the dog comfortable and, if bleeding is severe, apply a tourniquet above the wound, or apply a pressure bandage if the bleeding is less severe. Get to a veterinary surgery with all haste. A hospital will have a trained nurse available even if the vet is out on a call. Cover or wrap the patient in a coat or blanket to prevent heat loss and reduce shock.

Above: *To help stop blood loss in an emergency, it is advisable to apply a cold water compress to the wound first, and then apply a pressure bandage to distribute the pressure evenly.*

Below: *Bee stings are often visible, protruding through the coat from the skin. They can be removed with care, as shown here, using a magnifying glass and forceps (tweezers).*

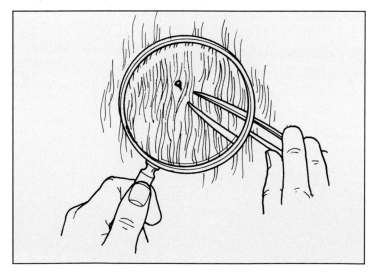

Chapter Five

BREEDING

Preliminaries
The mating
The pregnant bitch
Preparation for whelping
Care of mother bitch
Puppies' development and care
Worming
Nails and dew claws

Most people buying a puppy in the first instance are acquiring it for companionship and as an addition to their family life, and it is often not until some time later that it occurs to them that, if it is a bitch, they would like her to have puppies. Some feel that it may calm a lively bitch down, or be good for her and save her from problems later on, but these ideas have not been substantiated by breeders, or by the veterinary profession.

PRELIMINARIES

Breeding methods

There are three basic ways of breeding, which a knowledgeable stud dog owner would be able to explain to you in detail.

Inbreeding is where relationships of other dogs in the pedigree are quite close: you would recognize names that are the same in both pedigrees, very closely linked behind the parents of the proposed mating. Much experience is needed for inbreeding, as each parent passes on his or her own genetically good and bad faults in equal parts.

Out-crossing is where dogs are not related at all, and is only used by a breeder who feels that the lines are already very much inbred, and wants to introduce new blood to improve on certain characteristics.

Line breeding is the commonest method, where selection is directed towards the genetic points most desirable in both parents. Line breeding is where similar dogs appear further back in the pedigree — perhaps as far as grand- or great-grandparents.

The bitch's suitability

You need to cast a critical eye over your bitch, and consider several important factors. She may well have some very nice characteristics to pass on, and going to a good stud dog can certainly help to improve on many things from her, but remember the dog cannot be responsible for everything.

Did you buy her originally solely as a pet and decide to breed later? If so, was she specifically sold as good potential to breed from? Or were you advised not to breed from her? Does she have any particular trait or undesirable habit that you would not wish to perpetuate, and have you had anybody else pass an opinion on her worth as a breeding bitch? Is she in peak condition and capable of supporting on average eight to ten puppies?

The age that your bitch should have puppies depends on how mature she is mentally. If she is skittish and immature, she may not settle down to rear them happily. This can create many difficulties for any breeder, and certainly trauma in the bitch at her first attempt. Certainly she should not be bred from before 18 months of age, and it would probably be better between two and three years. If she is as much as four years old, perhaps a frank discussion with you veterinarian will enable you to decide whether or not she would be suitable as a brood bitch, and to prepare for any potential problems. Remember that both bitch and dog must be fully Kennel Club registered, otherwise puppies of the mating cannot be registered.

Time and cost entailed

Perhaps the following might be considered before proceeding. Firstly, there is the time and expense involved in producing a litter. Essentially, the owner needs to be at home most of the day, every day, to supervise the bitch during the last week of her pregnancy, and a great deal of time and attention must be given to the puppies as they are growing.

The first cost is x-raying the bitch to make sure she is sound enough to be bred from (see Chapter Three on Hip Dysplasia) and to have her eyes certified as being clear of Progressive Retinal Atrophy and Hereditary Cataract (see Chapter Three). Next is the stud dog fee and when the bitch has got over the first six weeks of her pregnancy, there will be three weeks of extra feeding for her, added to veterinary fees and

Above: *A bitch must be in peak condition if she is to produce healthy puppies. If she is fat and lethargic, she may not have enough stamina to cope.*

extra food again for six more weeks for the bitch, in addition to all the food that the puppies are going to need.

So, understandably, you have to prepare yourself for a big outlay, and the possibility of only a small proportion being recoverable from the venture. Of course, nobody dreams of including the cost of electricity, bedding, heat lamps, wire pens to keep growing puppies in, wear and tear and all the physical energy you put into the effort.

However, if you think you have put enough thought into the project, and you are sure it is not going to coincide with, for example, a forthcoming family holiday and that you can accommodate any unsold puppies until you find homes, it would be a good idea to ask an experienced breeder where you can find a suitable stud dog.

All your decisions should be made in good time, long before your bitch comes into season. You might like to go to a championship show or two to look at the best dogs for possible stud — and if so, try to see their progeny as well. A show catalogue will indicate quite a selection.

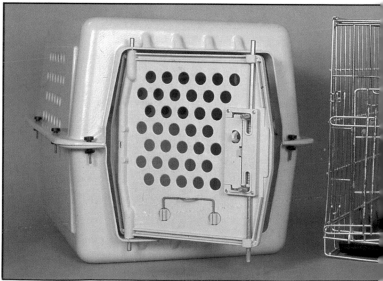

The stud dog

If you have difficulty in meeting experienced breeders in your search for a good dog, apply to the secretaries of the Labrador breed clubs who will be able to recommend suitable dogs. Your kennel club will have lists of established breeders and stud dog owners.

It is also sound practice to visit the home of the dog of your choice, to see his relatives and discuss the matching of your bitch's pedigree with that of the dog. All this must be arranged by prior appointment, and the owner of the dog will probably be interested to see your bitch and to be informed about the results of her eye examination and X-rays (see Chapter Three on Hip Dysplasia) and will give you those of the dog.

Never use a friend's dog because he or she wants you to, and you both think that he is a nice dog. He may never have established that he really has something to pass on, and the average puppy buyer will certainly want to know about the father. Most people like to see winning parents on the pedigree. Also difficulties might arise in trying to mate them if both dogs are inexperienced.

Finally, having used the dog next door, he may never be used again, and you may have left your neighbour with a dog that will howl every time any other neighbourhood bitch comes into season.

Of course, if your choice is that of a well-known winning champion in the breed, you will have to be sure that his owner feels that your bitch is good enough.

THE MATING

The usual procedure is for the bitch to be taken to the stud dog to be served, usually around the twelfth to fourteenth day of her season — that is, counting from the first day that she shows a coloured discharge, the owner having previously notified the stud dog owner of the onset of the bitch's season so that the stud dog is sure to be available for that day.

If you plan to send your bitch to the dog by air, a common practice in the USA, arrangements with the airline must be made well in advance. A crate must be acquired and the stud dog owner will meet your bitch on arrival at the airport, probably a few days before she is due to be bred, and will return her to you, of course, after the mating has been achieved.

I like to check that the bitch has been 'swinging her tail' over her back, and flirting with females for at least two days, before taking her to the stud. If she is showing dark red colour and her vulva is still rather hard to touch, the mating perhaps could be postponed for a couple of days. It is always tempting to rush off to the dog in case the bitch's season goes over, and this happens to the most experienced, but usually a bitch will stand to be mated for four or five days at least, and the

Left: *This excellent show dog produced both fine working dogs and show champions. Puppies from such dogs train well as companions.*

Below: *Dogs enjoy the security of plastic crates or collapsible wire cages. These are useful both in the home and when travelling.*

later she is left the more likely it is that the ova will have travelled down to the uterus for union with the sperm.

A stud dog owner who has a few dogs at stud may well be operating single-handedly, and naturally wishes to give as much attention to each individual as possible. He or she will therefore appreciate your co-operation, so keep the appointment as arranged, and the stud dog owner will advise you whether or not the bitch is ready.

Take a stout leather collar and a good lead with you and let your bitch have a short walk on the lead before arriving at your destination. When you do arrive, leave her in the car with a window only slightly open, while you get out and make your presence known to the stud dog owner.

Do not allow her to urinate near or on the stud dog owner's premises, which will attract local dogs or give any other studs on the property a scent of the bitch, with the possible result that they will spend the night howling.

A well organised stud will have an appropriate place for the mating, usually well away from other dogs. You will probably be asked to put the collar on your bitch quite tightly, and to take her to the appointed spot. The dog of your choice will be brought out on a lead, and it is very important that the bitch is not allowed to snap at the dog.

If she is 'ready' to be mated, she will stand still and swing her tail over for the dog. She will stand four-square with ears pricked up and her eyes will be bright and alert. If she is frightened or nervous, or not ready, she will sit down with her tail between her legs and maybe snap at the dog. These are classic signs that she needs a couple more days.

Occasionally, with lots of encouragement from both dog and owner, she may eventually stand, but otherwise, if she runs behind her owner, it is better to leave her a couple of days. Some bitches prefer to be free and run around — but this can be fairly exhausting for the stud dog.

If a mating is not effected you will be asked to return in two days' time, when you will probably find that the bitch is only too willing to accept the dog.

A good stud dog will mount and mate a bitch within a few minutes, and then turn and stand back to back with the bitch for about 20 minutes. After they separate the bitch should be returned to the car, and you should remember to loosen her collar. The dog will be returned to his kennel by his owner.

You will be given a receipt for the stud fee, a pedigree of the dog you used, a Kennel Club form signed by the owner of the stud dog with his name, Kennel Club registration and date of mating written on it, and possibly a diet sheet for a bitch in whelp and one for the puppies to come.

It is the custom that if the bitch fails to conceive, there is a free repeat mating the following season. This is not legally binding, and the owner of the bitch pays for the service of the dog, not for the ensuing puppies.

THE PREGNANT BITCH

For the first six weeks of the pregnancy, your bitch's routine will remain the same as usual. Perhaps after three weeks she could have an extra egg and milk feed, plus some calcium additive in her daily meal. Often, after two or three weeks she may become more affectionate, and at the same time her nipples may appear to turn slightly more pink. At five weeks her ribcage may appear to be slightly heavier, and often after her meal a slight fullness between the end of her ribs and her loin will be evident.

Three weeks before her proposed whelping time — which is approximately 63 days, if in whelp — she will need at least an extra pound (450g) of meat per day, and if heavy in whelp by the eighth week, another additional pound of meat, chicken or fish per day will be required. There is no need to increase her normal biscuit meal intake.

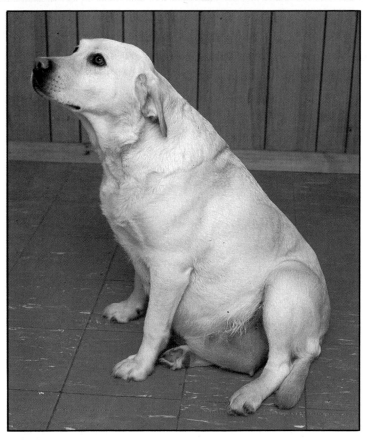

Above: *A bitch four days before her eight puppies were born. Gentle exercise is fine, but avoid car travel because of jolts.*

Below: *Pregnant bitches will lie around the house with their heads between their paws. They may also express milk.*

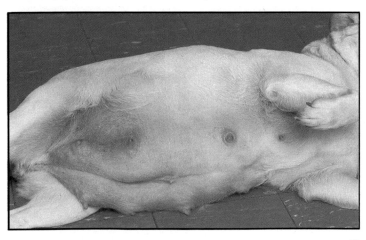

PREPARATION FOR WHELPING

You need to plan in advance where you would like your bitch to have her puppies — inside or out? Inside, perhaps you will choose the utility room, extension or kitchen — or certainly somewhere warm, with a radiator or electrical supply, where you can suspend a heat lamp. Outside, an outbuilding or shed that is well insulated and has an electrical supply is quite suitable.

The whelping box

Your bitch at first needs a box, about 3ft (1m) square with sides at least 18in (50cm) high and floor covered with many layers of newspaper. I like to put a table over the box and throw a big double blanket over all, which makes a cosy nest, free from draughts. Then there is no need for a heat lamp. An alternative to a table is a wire garden compost pen which will come in handy later for keeping puppies restricted to a confined area rather like a play-pen. With three sides round the box, and one side attached over the top, you then put the blanket, etc over all.

——— Equipment ———

Newspapers in abundance
Terry-towel nappies or rough
  Turkish towelling
Kitchen paper
Scissors
Thermometer for room
  temperature
Clinical thermometer for the bitch
Blanket
Torch
Infra-red lamp
Hot water bottle and cover
Cardboard carton

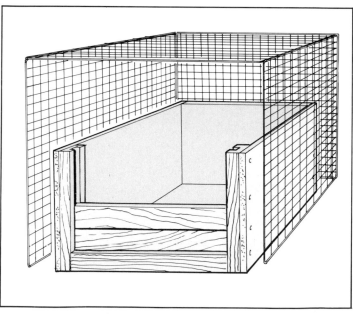

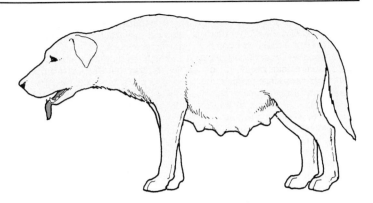

Above: *Immediately before whelping the bitch will start to pant and look distressed. She may refuse her food or be sick. Give her lots of attention.*

Left: *A heat lamp suspended over the whelping box provides warmth for the puppies during and after whelping.*

Below left: *The whelping box should be 3ft (91cm) square with a lower, removable front. A blanket draped over the wire pen will make a warm, cosy nest.*

If the lamp is to be used, arrange to suspend it from a bracket for the lamp to hang 3ft (91cm) above the whelping box. A constant temperature of 75°F (24°C) is needed for the first few days in the area where the puppies are kept, because they cannot control their own body temperature for the first week, and are solely dependent on heat from their mother's body, with any surrounding draughts eliminated. Puppies lying in a heap huddled up are cold, and those lying flat out spaced all over the box are too hot.

A few days before your bitch is due, encourage her to sleep in the box, and within 48 hours of whelping, she will probably begin to scratch up the newspapers that you placed inside. It is far better to accustom her to the designated place, or she will search for her own spot anywhere in the house.

Similarly, if you must confine her outside, restrict her occasionally to the prepared chosen shed or stable, and keep an eye on her. She may decide to scratch up all the earth under another garden shed!

The whelping
Although 63 days gestation is quoted as the norm, in fact bitches can whelp quite happily a few days before or after the estimated date.

The first signs that she may be about to whelp are searching around, panting and scratching up to make a nest, milk when teats are pressed, and obvious discomfort. She may get a little fussy about her meals, and they may need to be divided into six instead of three per day. She may have a colourless mucous discharge, due to the weight of the puppies. This is quite normal.

Her rectal temperature, usually around 101°F will begin to drop to 99°F (38.5-37°C) two or three days before whelping begins, and will drop further on the day or night of the event. By this time she will be urinating more often, will pant harder and harder, and will begin to look distressed and keep looking towards her tail. Her temperature may drop to 98°F (36.5°C) or lower, and she will begin a process of muscular rippling to move puppies gently towards the vulva.

Now, if you watch closely, she may begin to contract; or you may hear a grunt or two — and this is the moment to note down the exact time. When she goes outside at night, always follow with a torch. You may find that she thought her contraction was a desire to open her bowels, and that she drops a puppy instead. Contractions begin occurring at increasingly regular intervals, and she will confine herself to her new box. Occasionally a bitch will prefer to whelp somewhere other than in the box. I think it is better to let her please herself. Once the first puppy is born, it is easy to take it and put it into the whelping box where she will then stay.

She probably refused her latest meal. Maybe she will be sick, and she is probably going around in ever-increasing circles! Finally, there is a big heave, and you will see what you might think is a balloon protruding from her vulva. This is making way for the first puppy. She will turn around and clean up the fluid that the bag enveloped, and after a few more contractions the puppy will be visible.

Help and encouragement from you is urgently needed at this stage

Below: *Once the puppies have been licked clean by the bitch, place them by her nipples and encourage them to suck as this stimulates uterine contractions.*

— remember, it is all new to her, and her instincts must be allowed to take precedence.

The bitch must be encouraged to lick the bag that the puppy is born in. The placenta should be delivered next, and the bitch will eat it nipping the cord, and finally starting to lick the puppy.

At this point, I like to remove the bag from around the puppy's face, and rub along its back with a towel to encourage a cry and make it take a breath. It is at this point that the maternal circulation through the placenta to the puppy has to change to heart-lung circulation in the puppy itself.

Encourage the puppy (who will move around in anti-clockwise circles) to get into its mother's breast and suck, which encourages the uterus to contract. Usually, within 20 minutes another puppy will be on the way. Note the time each puppy is born, whether the placenta was delivered and what time the next contractions began.

The bitch should continue to have her puppies at reasonably regular intervals. Occasionally (and with a big litter she may pause for a long rest of perhaps an hour or so), she can be persuaded to relieve herself and perhaps have a drink of warm

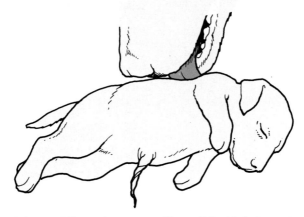

Above: *If the bitch does not immediately accept and lick her puppies, keep them warm, and she should accept them later.*

milk and glucose. Afterwards, encourage her to go out again to relieve herself, and while you are outside with her, ask somebody else to replace all the newspapers with clean ones ready for her to settle on. Offer her more milk and perhaps half a pound (250g) of her favourite meat, but do not worry if she refuses.

It is a good idea to have asked your veterinarian to call in as soon as it is convenient for him or her, or the following morning to check that there are no puppies or afterbirths left inside the mother, and to check the puppies over and make sure they are all sound.

Possible problems
You do need to be aware of one or two danger signals that show all is not well. Contractions should not go on for more than 1½ hours without a puppy being delivered. Contact your veterinarian if they do, and be prepared to give him accurate details of the whelping so far.

Occasionally, a maiden bitch will clam up in sheer fright, or some may show a green discharge, sign of a late arrival. You may be asked to take the bitch in to the surgery where facilities for investigation are far better than in your home. Sometimes the journey itself can cause a bitch to deliver in the car, so it is best to take with you newspaper, towels and a companion. Leave the other puppies on a well wrapped up hot water

bottle, inside a carton, under the heat lamp.

Some puppies live for three days or so, and then suddenly give up, probably through some malfunction of the heart. Some are born much smaller than the rest, but are quite determined to live, are very active and agile, and although smaller at birth may, by the end of the year, have grown to the size of their litter-mates.

Finally, it is usual to let your veterinarian see your bitch if she goes more than two days over the due date. Provided that there is no discharge and that she is eating and not being sick, and seems to be perfectly happy with herself, she can, in fact, go quite a few days longer — but, of course, it is sensible to allow an expert to keep an eye on her.

Occasionally there may be a weak puppy that does not want to suck, and cries forlornly. It may have a cleft palate, or a defective valve in the heart or a blockage through an unseen malformation. If the cries upset the bitch, take the puppy well out of her hearing, possibly to the veterinarian for disposal. Bitches instinctively know when a puppy should not be allowed to live.

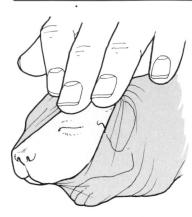

Above: *Gently remove the 'water bag' membrane from the puppy, if the mother does not do so, as soon as it is born.*

Sometimes, when a puppy is born, it appears to be dead. Get the bag off its face and quickly, but gently, rub it with a towel to promote circulation.

Warming carefully under the lamp and tossing movements from hand to hand can sometimes revive it, or pulling its tongue gently forward — even blowing into its lungs very gently, along with gentle massage over the rib cage, can sometimes accelerate breathing.

You can work for 15 minutes or more in this manner, and may well be rewarded with a gasp or other sign of life, but it is wise to remember that the longer the brain is left without oxygen, the less likely is the chance of survival for the puppy.

As more and more puppies are being born, it is useful to have a second cardboard box with a well wrapped hot water bottle in it, to put the earlier-born puppies in. This gives the bitch more room to manoeuvre in the whelping box.

Always remember to return the puppies to her at the first convenient moment, however, or you may turn your back for a minute and then find that she has got out of her cardboard box and is trying to squeeze into the little cardboard box with them!!

CARE OF THE MOTHER BITCH

Diet

For the first three days food should be lighter than usual, perhaps reducing the meat, chicken or fish to 8oz (200g) twice daily. I recommend tinned rice pudding, diluted with equal water in small quantities over the day.

Most bitches can look after eight or nine puppies well, but will also need a large amount of protein and calcium to help them cope. Therefore you must constantly increase the amount of food, and even when the puppies are a week old, she will need at least 3lb (1.5kg) of meat daily.

A condition called eclampsia, that occurs only rarely in the Labrador, is brought on by a lack of calcium, and is quite dangerous. It can be avoided by making sure that the bitch's calcium intake is sufficient in the form of milk and proprietary calcium/phosphate powders.

From three weeks of age the puppies will take less from their

mother as you begin feeding them and care must be taken that you gradually reduce the amount of food offered.

Prevention and treatment of mastitis

The bitch's milk glands really do not fill up very much until the third day, and overfeeding before then could make them swell and become purplish and very uncomfortable. Although the puppies appear to be suckling almost all the time, the actual amount of milk they take is very small. If the bitch is given too much fluid, she will develop mastitis (inflammation of the breast), where the nipples become so pronounced and breasts so swollen, that the puppies cannot suck from them. Although antiobiotics rapidly take down the inflammation, they can also have a loosening effect on the small puppies' bowels, so this problem is to be avoided at all costs, although it can occur again when the puppies are being weaned.

If mastitis looks like developing, I recommend soaking some thin towelling in boiling water, squeezing it out and applying it as a compress. If it can be held in your own hand, the temperature will be bearable for the bitch. Gently massage each affected breast until the milk flows freely again.

Separation from the litter

When making arrangements for the departure of puppies, it is kinder to the mother to stagger it over a few days. When they have all gone, she will again be free to go out with you for walks, and enjoy extra comforts as a reward for her efforts.

When the puppies are about 12 weeks old, the bitch will cast her coat and lose the feather on her tail. She will look thin and dreadful — but do not despair. Her coat will grow in again, and in two months she will be looking her old self.

Below: *If the bitch shows signs of feeling strange at the sight of her new puppies, try to get someone to cradle her head while each puppy suckles.*

PUPPIES' DEVELOPMENT AND CARE

Puppies grow quite rapidly, and it is quite instructive to weigh each puppy daily and make a chart of the recorded weights, in order to plot their progression over the first few weeks of life. At birth they weigh between 1lb and 1lb 4oz (450-600g) and usually gain 2oz (50g) a day. In a week they should double their birth weight.

After another week the puppies become more interesting, and you will notice that their mother begins to leave them alone for short periods of time.

At two weeks puppies will be able to hear, their eyes will begin to open, they can move quite well round the whelping box or their bed, and they are beginning to hear noises.

By three weeks of age they will start to find their feet, and will gravitate towards sights and sounds. They should weigh 4 to 4½ lb (1.75-2kg). By four weeks they will

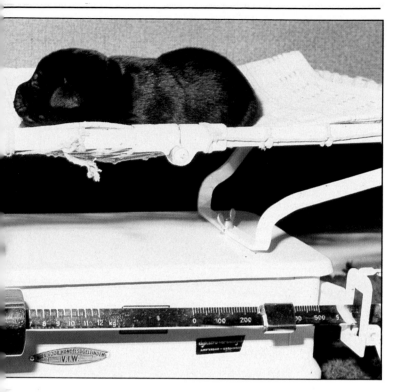

Above: *Small puppies can be weighed on kitchen scales or spring balance scales which are more stable and more accurate. Watch for any decline in weight.*

Left: *New born puppies can neither see nor hear, but after a fortnight or so they will be able to hear, their eyes will start to open, and they will move around their box.*

be barking and playing a little with each other. They can co-ordinate enough to stand and feed from a dish.

By about six weeks they should weigh 8 to 10lb (3.5-4.5kg) and by eight weeks nearer 12lb (5.5kg). Some, of course, thrive extremely well and are a lot heavier; but it must be remembered that their boney framework — or skeleton — is hardly true bone until nearly six months, and you are putting a great deal of strain on the muscles, ligaments and unformed bones if the

puppy becomes over-fat.

You may like to record all their growing data to compare, perhaps, with a subsequent litter.

Do not be tempted to allow lots of people to come in and handle new puppies. Germs can so easily be transmitted on clothes, and especially on footwear, and although the puppies carry a fair amount of natural maternal immunity, it is always safer to ask people to view from a distance, however eager they are to pick them up and cuddle them.

Feeding
Begin weaning at three weeks by liquidizing ½ teaspoonful of finely minced high quality tinned dog food or meat without fat per puppy, and gradually increase daily intake to ½oz (14g) of meat per puppy given over two feeds, or ½lb (200g) for the whole litter (on average between eight and ten puppies).

However, it is difficult to generalize about feeding. A puppy

Diet chart for approximately 8 young puppies

3-4 weeks: Gradually increase the 1lb (450g) meat fed in two feeds, for whole litter. Give a taste of liquidized rice pudding with an equal amount of water in the middle of the day.

4-5 weeks: Increase meat to 1½lb (700g) per day, divided into two or three meals. Intersperse with rice pudding and perhaps give a cereal breakfast and milk. Start adding a teaspoonful of soaked puppy meal to each meat feed.

5-6 weeks: 3oz (100g) meat and ½ teaspoon puppy meal per feed daily **for each puppy.** Continue with three daily milk meals. Feed each puppy separately.

6-7 weeks: Three meat feeds increasing from 4-6oz (113-170g) per feed. One teaspoon increasing to one tablespoon of soaked puppy meal or meat feed. One teaspoon of calcium additive in first meat feed. Plus two milk feeds of 5oz (142g) of rice pudding with equal water.

7-8 weeks: 8oz (227g) meat plus one tablespoon of soaked puppy meal fed three times a day. Two milk feeds of 7oz (199g) of rice pudding with equal water.

that is bigger than average — say 1lb 4oz (600g) is going to be able to eat more at three weeks than a puppy that weighed only 10-12oz (300-350g) at birth. See the diet chart on page 78 for a guideline to feeding puppies up to eight weeks.

Puppies should be fed separately from four weeks, and given lots of individual attention.

At any time during weaning or even later, as the puppies are growing on, a slight deviation of diet may cause sloppy motions, leading to diarrhoea. These motions may be

Below: *Take care not to give puppies too much food to begin with, and from about four weeks feed them separately.*

caused by worm infestation, but the cause is more likely to be intolerance of fatty food. If this is not noticed and is neglected, the motions will begin to take on a grey colour, and it is quite likely that the digestive organs have been upset.

Although it might be tempting to feed a milky diet, it is preferable to cook fish or chicken, and offer this in small quantities followed, if tolerated, by the addition of boiled rice. Meanwhile, try to work out what changes in feeding have caused the digestive upset. Exclude the offending food, and gradually return to a normal diet.

A dietary upset, at its worst, can cause permanent damage to the pancreas (the organ that produces some of the enzymes for digestion).

WORMING

I like to start worming my puppies at three weeks of age. I always use tablets supplied by my veterinarian, and weigh each puppy to establish the dosage. I follow this procedure weekly, noting down the dates and results for future reference, up to six weeks of age.

It is highly advisable to plan a worming programme in consultation with your veterinarian (see page 32 for information on roundworms).

When worming the puppies, it is a good idea to worm the mother also on the first occasion.

NAILS AND DEW CLAWS

Many breeders like to have front dew claws removed when puppies are three days old. There should not be any dew claws on the hind legs, and removal must not be carried out by an inexperienced person, but left to a veterinarian.

Toe nails will require trimming, because they soon grow like hooks that latch on to the bitch's skin round the teats and hurt a lot, so trimming each week helps to prevent soreness. Be very careful when trimming the nails not to clip too far up the nail into the fleshy part, known as the quick (see page 36 for further advice on clipping nails).

Chapter Six

SHOWING

Breed Standards
The show dog
Training for showing
Conformation
Types of show
Show procedures

BREED STANDARDS

For the breed to succeed and be recognized by the Kennel Clubs in the UK and USA, a standard (or ideal) of the breed had to be created. This helped to encourage breeders of both field trial and show dogs to try to aim at improving the pure-bred dog.

UK Standard

The general appearance has to be that of a strongly built dog, short coupled, very active, with a broad skull, broad and deep through the chest and ribs, broad and strong over the loins and hindquarters.

Characteristics Good tempered, very agile, with an excellent nose, soft mouth and keen love of water. An adaptable and devoted companion.

Temperament Intelligent, keen and biddable, with a strong will to please. A kindly nature, with no aggression or undue shyness.

Head A broad skull with a defined stop. Clean-cut, without fleshy cheeks. Jaws of medium length, powerful not snipey. Nose wide, nostrils well-developed. Neat stop between the eyes.

Eyes Medium size, not bold or prominent, expressing intelligence and good temper, brown or hazel.

Ears Not large or heavy, hanging close to head and set rather far back.

Mouth Jaws and teeth strong with a perfect, regular and complete scissor bite — that is, upper teeth closely overlapping lower teeth and set square into the jaws.

Neck Clean, strong, powerful, set into well-placed shoulders.

Forequarters Shoulders long and sloping. Forelegs well-boned and straight from elbow to ground when viewed from either front or side.

Body Chest of good width and depth, with well-sprung barrel ribs. Level topline. Hocks wide, short-coupled and strong.

Below: *A well-proportioned dog, powerfully built to withstand a day's work in the field.*

Above: *With her well-formed head, this yellow bitch looks alert and intelligent. Note also her thick, weather-resistant coat.*

Hindquarters Well-developed, not sloping to tail. Well-turned stifle. Hocks well let down. Cowhocks highly undesirable.
Feet Round, compact; well-arched toes and well-developed pads.
Tail Distinctive feature, very thick towards base, gradually tapering towards tip, medium length, free from feathering, but clothed thickly all round with short, thick, dense coat, thus giving rounded appearance — described as otter tail. May be carried gaily, but should not curl over back.
Gait/movement Free, covering adequate ground, straight and true in front and rear.
Coat Distinctive feature of the breed. Dense topcoat with fairly harsh texture; slightly woolly and dense undercoat completely covering the skin, when you turn the top hair back. Short and dense without wave or feathering, giving fairly hard feel to the touch. Weather resistant undercoat.
Colour Wholly black, yellow or liver/chocolate. Yellows range from light cream to fox red. Small white spot on chest permissible.
Size Height at withers:
Dogs — 22-22 ½ in (56-57cm).
Bitches — 21 ½ in (54-56cm).
  Faults are listed as bad mouths, poor coats, bad movement, feathering, snipiness on the head, large and heavy ears, and cowhocks. The seriousness with which the fault is regarded, should be in exact proportion to its degree.
Note: Male animals should have two apparently normal testicles fully descended into the scrotum.

US Standard
General appearance Same as for UK standard
Head The stop need only be slightly pronounced, so that the skull is not absolutely in a straight line with the nose.
Teeth To be set level in the mouth.
Eyes Can be brown, yellow or black, but brown or black preferred.
Coat Gives no mention of undercoat. Colour: Blacks: black or yellow eyes are permissible. Yellows: varying from fox red to light cream, with variations in the shading of the coat or ears and underparts of the dog, or beneath its tail. Eye colour should be that of the blacks, with black or dark brown eye rims. The nose should be black or dark brown — although fading to pink in winter weather is not serious. A 'Dudley' nose (pink without pigmentation) should be penalized. Chocolates: shades ranging from Light Sedge to Chocolate. A small white spot on the chest is permissible. Eyes to be light brown to clear yellow. Nose and eye-rim pigmentation dark brown or liver coloured. Fading to pink in winter weather not serious. 'Dudley' nose should be penalized.
Movement Should be free and effortless.
Forelegs Should be strong, straight and true, and correctly placed. In a

dog moving towards you, the elbows should not be out in front, but neatly held to the body with legs not too close together, and moving straight forward without pacing or weaving. Viewing the dog from the rear, you should get the impression that the hind legs, which should be well muscled and not cowhocked, move as nearly parallel as possible, with hocks doing their full share of the work and flexing well — thus giving the appearance of power and strength.

Size Dogs 22½ in (57.5-62cm) at shoulder; 69-75lb (31.5-34kg). Bitches 21½-23½ in (55-60cm) 55-70lb (25-32kg).

The rest of the breed standard is similar to that of the UK standard given on pages 82-3.

THE SHOW DOG

A show dog should be as near to the breed standard as possible, with correct eye colour, double waterproof coat of correct texture, good bone and substance, typical head, feet and an otter tail. There are, of course, many types within a breed, and a dog will win at a show according to what the judge's eyes see and prefer.

The choice of a possible show puppy depends on the experience and judgement of those making the selection, using the knowledge they have acquired over the years of how a puppy is going to develop. Obviously, parentage counts a great deal, and just as the best field trial dogs come from proven field trial winners, I think it is the same with potential show specimens.

Perhaps you have chosen to buy a potential show puppy instead of a breeding bitch, preferably from a well-established and reputable

Below: *American breeders have used imported English stock to bring their Labradors closer to the UK standard.*

Above: *A promising puppy of five months shows his good points in a typical show stance.*

breeder, who will be only too willing to try to guide you along the right lines. Make sure tho breeder knows that you would like to show the puppy if it turns out to be good enough. Nobody can guarantee that it will, but a breeder should at least be able to make an educated guess about your puppy's show potential.

The dog must be fit, having had enough, but not too much, road walking. It must carry exactly the right amount of weight, be in as good coat as possible, with a nice gloss on top and well groomed.

I always feel sorry for people who have obviously bought a puppy as a pet, take it in to the ring and show it, complete with the faults that caused it to be sold as a pet in the first place.

Your first entry into the show ring may well be a personal embarrassment to you, but people are generally kind and helpful and in no time at all you will feel accepted. Ringcraft classes are a great help in socializing a puppy in the pre-show months, and will help you to overcome any inhibitions you may have.

Once you become involved in showing, and have a few wins, a new world opens up to you. There is a great deal of thrill and satisfaction attached to winning, but understandably there can be disappointments too, when inevitably, sometimes you lose.

TRAINING FOR SHOWING

For those who are not near such facilities as ringcraft, training must begin at home. Learning to walk on a show lead around the garden daily, without pulling — perhaps using a check chain to make the dog heel is fine to begin with. Practise standing still, making it look towards you — this can be done in the house, and preferably in front of a mirror — to see just how it is standing and whether its back legs are properly positioned, or whether it is dipping its top line. Always 'go over' your dog after standing it; teach it to stay still to have its teeth and bite looked at. Use your hands, as the judge does, feeling its spring of rib, bones and feet; go over the rump, tail, and so get it used generally to being systematically judged. Then praise it and give a reward. Next move it up and down the room or garden, keeping its attention on you alone. Always make it fun and from three months of age it will come to look forward to being shown.

85

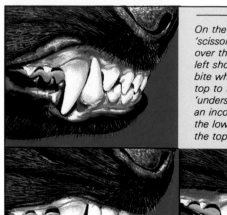

Bites

On the left is the correct 'scissor' bite; the top teeth fit over the bottom teeth. Below left shows the incorrect 'level' bite where the front teeth meet top to top. Below shows the 'undershot' mouth. This is also an incorrect bite. In this case the lower teeth go in front of the top teeth.

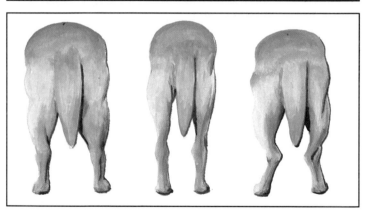

Above: *The hindquarters on the left are correct — strong and muscular with hocks slightly bent. The middle and right are both incorrect — narrow and weak; cow-hocked respectively.*

Below: *The heads left and middle are incorrect — muzzle on left is upturned; middle is narrow and weak. The head on right is correct — a broad skull, pronounced stop and wide nose.*

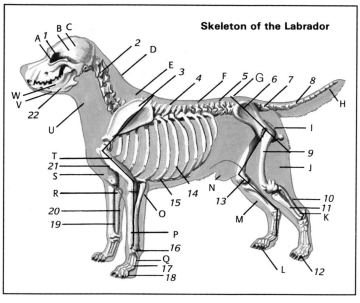

Skeleton of the Labrador

Skeleton
*1 Skull 2 Neck vertebrae 3 Scapula
4 Thoracic vertebrae 5 Lumber
vertebrae 6 Pelvis 7 Sacrum
8 Coccygeal vertebrae 9 Femur
10 Fibula 11 Tibia 12 Hind digits
13 Patella 14 Ribs 15 Sternum
16 Carpus 17 Metacarpals 18 Front
digits 19 Radius 20 Ulna 21
Humerus 22 Mandible (lower jaw)*

Conformation points
A Stop B Forehead C Occiput
D Nape E Withers F Back G Croup
H Tail or Stern I Loins J Thigh
K Hock L Toes M Stifle N Sheath
O Elbow P Forearm Q Pastern
R Brisket S Chest T Shoulder
U Throat V Lower jaw and flews
W Cheek

The diagram also shows the
correct shoulder and hind
angulation (a 90° angle at the
shoulder joint; 145° at the elbow).

Top left: *The tail illustrated here is
set too low.*

Centre left: *The tail must not curl
over the back as here.*

Bottom left: *An illustration of the
correct set of tail.*

TYPES OF SHOW

UK
It is important to understand the types of shows that there are. There are the small village Exemption shows, where you enter on the day, and the once-monthly Dog Matches held by the local society's ringcraft classes. Then there are the sanction and limited shows held for members of the local canine societies. Open shows are often held in conjunction with agricultural societies in the summer, with usually four to six classes for each breed. The open breed shows, too, with perhaps 20 classes, are excellent bases for learning a lot more about your breed and fellow exhibitors in your area.

The general Championship shows, again with often 20 breed classes on offer, are where you can reach your goal, the Challenge Certificates awarded by the Kennel Club. Included also are the Breed Society and Gundog Society Championship shows, with similar classification.

These championship shows are the ultimate in the show world, because a win of best bitch or best dog in breed gives the coveted Challenge Certificate. Three Challenge Certificates under three different judges gives the title 'Show Champion' to the dog or bitch concerned. It may take four years or more to achieve this goal, and only a small percentage of winning exhibits rise to these heights each year.

Once the Best of Breed has been awarded for each individual breed competing in the show, these winners go on to compete in their 'group' before being considered for the top award, Best in Show. In the UK, all breeds are divided into six groups, the Labrador being a member of the Gundog group.

USA
In America the classification at

Below: *A judge's job is much easier when dogs are well handled and attentive.*

Left: *Dogs should be taught to sit or lie quietly on their bench during a show and not be a nuisance to neighbours.*

shows is different, as there are not so many breed classes and fewer varieties of shows. First, there is the sanctioned match, which is an informal meeting of pure-bred dogs in competition, and can be held by any club. This is very useful for gaining show experience.

The main type of show is either a speciality show for one breed, or the general regional show at top level, which offers puppy, novice, bred by exhibitor, American-bred, and open classes for each sex. Champions have a separate class, and the dogs earn points towards their titles through wins out of the classes, in competition for best of winners, and placings in the ultimate groups. There are seven groups in all — the Labrador is in the Sporting group.

SHOW PROCEDURES

Weekly dog papers advertise forthcoming shows and venues, and to enter, you apply to the secretaries of societies for schedules and entry forms.

It would be advisable to begin by exhibiting at small local shows where you and your dog can get the feel of things. Always allow plenty of time for travelling to shows, because some venues can be in the most out-of-the-way places.

The night before the show, you will need to check your schedule which will tell you the time and place of judging. You should have a bag or hold-all ready for brushes, combs, towels, talcum powder, glossy coat spray, chamois leather, show lead, benching chain and collar, ring number holder, bowl, water, and perhaps dog food. You may like to pack a picnic for yourself, and maybe items of first-aid equipment for cuts and stings — and, importantly, a poopa-scoopa!

It is preferable to stop during your journey and exercise your dog adequately, to prevent it fouling the

show venue. Areas around and inside show venues being fouled by dogs often leads to venues being lost to dog shows through complaints in the neighbourhood.

If you are entering your dog in a Championship show, it will have to be trained to sit on its bench quietly, with its collar and chain attached to the appropriate holding ring.

Once you have taken the plunge, and got yourself into the ring, watch carefully to see what everybody else is doing. Remember that it is the dog that the judge is going to look at, not you. The ring steward will give you your ring number, and you will present your dog in line for the judge to see. You may be asked to move around the ring at a steady trot. Then you wait in line for the judge to 'go over' each dog individually.

Once you get up to the judge, make sure that you present your dog to its best advantage. Listen to the judge when he asks you to move your dog — be it straight up and down, or in the form of a triangle. Then return to the line. When the individual judging is completed, you will be required to stand your dog once again and bait it to present the best possible profile.

If you feed titbits (highly recommended to keep Labradors' concentration), be careful that you do not annoy or interfere with the exhibits on either side of you. You should always congratulate the winner of the class, as this shows good sportsmanship.

In Labradors competition is very high, and as there are so many breeders of long standing with some superb dogs, you really will have to be good to get to the top. This does not mean that you cannot enjoy great success, even if your exhibit is not up to championship level — for the beauty of showing is that you can always compete at the next level down and be a regular winner.

Perhaps, of course, your dog for some reason takes a dislike to the show ring, but all is not necessarily lost. He or she may prefer obedience training at a local society — or maybe gundog training (see Chapter

Six), where usually a Labrador's greatest talent lies, in order to satisfy your dog's natural instincts.

I think it is important that a dog enjoys the life you choose for it — and particularly in the gundog world, it may open up a whole new way of life for you, too.

The USA
In the USA many dog owners prefer to handle their own exhibits, but at most general shows the dogs are not

Above: *In a scene of a typical American show field, a beautiful yellow bitch poses with her Best of Breed trophies, the ribbons held by the English judge who awarded them.*

baited, and are prepared, groomed and handled rather differently. There is a big fraternity of professional handlers travelling the show circuits in huge pantechnicans, with as many as 30 dogs of all breeds in crates on board. They have wonderful facilities, and may be on the circuit for a week at a time, or more.

Occasionally, a show dog owner will keep her own dog, and meet up with her handler at an appointed show. The dogs are much more disciplined for exhibition than in England, and Americans visiting the show scene in the UK find it very much more relaxed.

91

Chapter Seven

WORKING LABRADORS

Gundogs
Guide dogs for the blind
PAT dogs
Hearing dogs for the deaf
Sniffer dogs
Devastation rescue teams

The Labrador, as a breed, has many qualities, as we have seen — a fine temperament, dependability, intelligence, agility, a keen sense of smell and a soft mouth. These characteristics have established it as one of the prime breeds to be trained and worked in the field as a gundog, as well as being trained for public service.

GUNDOGS

Very many exhibitors in the show world are unaware of the pleasures of owning and working a gundog. And yet almost every Labrador must be trainable to some degree, their great instinct to please and to retrieve having been bred in them for generations.

The Labrador first appeared in a field trial in 1904, and since that time has established itself as a firm retrieving favourite.

There is no doubt that a working dog gives immense satisfaction, and creates a true bond of unity between owner and dog. Those contemplating such an avenue are advised to join their local gundog club, where lessons are given in technique and the requirements for a working dog.

A working Labrador must be very fit and of the highest order of training. It has to have enough courage to enter thick bramble and retrieve from any situation; and be

Left: *Labradors are natural retrievers. A favourite lesson is being taught to retrieve dummies under a trainer's expert eye.*

Below: *The excitement never palls when the dog emerges from dense vegetation, having found the fallen bird solely by scent.*

Well-trained and active Labradors are often invited to follow the guns at syndicate shoots and 'pick up' the birds that the regular dogs have failed to find. The owners derive a great deal of pleasure from learning to work their dogs in this way, and if the dog shows exceptional aptitude, they may well go on to train the dog for the very demanding field trials run to test the ability and agility of the first-class gundog. However, years of dedication are needed for success in these trials.

able to scent game, and bring it back to its owner without dropping it. It is essential that it can work on its own initiative. Few show Labradors could ever compete for top honours at a field trial against the fast stylish Labradors bred specially for work.

Labradors make ideal companion dogs for the shooting syndicates. These sportsmen require well-trained dogs to own and take with them on game bird shoots: pheasant, partridge and snipe — many of which are reared for the winter by the landowners' gamekeepers.

Labradors and Chesapeake Bay Retrievers really come into their own in goose and duck shooting. The challenge is great. The need is for very hardy dogs with plenty of stamina and guts, because they are working in fast-flowing rivers, on muddy and slippery banks, and maybe standing for hours in icy-cold water, waiting to retrieve duck and goose for their masters.

Training

Preliminary training can be done at home, but anything as serious as retrieving, being steady to gunfire, and marking, is best taught by the specialists who voluntarily train classes at local gundog societies.

Apart from normal obedience work, your dog would be taught to watch dummies being thrown out and would retrieve them on command. It will become accustomed to gunfire, be taught to retrieve from water, and over water, as well as to jump fences and to retrieve dummies it did not see fall. There are working tests for novices and open tests; from these one can graduate to full field trials.

Often young dogs and grown on puppies respond more readily to obedience training working with dummies as it is applied in the field, rather than to straightforward class obedience.

Courses are usually weekly and it is very rewarding to have, with training, advanced to the point where your dog is one of a line of dogs sitting across the middle of a field, waiting to be called up to do a

Top: *A dog must first learn to watch where a dummy or buffer falls in water before swimming to retrieve the moving object.*

Above: *The dog's natural instinct is to retrieve the bird out of the water. It should then bring the bird direct to its owner's hand.*

retrieve. There are many handlers today whose original dogs did not come up to expectation in the show ring. They have found pleasure in learning to work their dogs, and have not only taken part in 'picking up' at local shoots, but have advanced to novice and open working tests and, eventually, the ultimate — field trials.

Field trials are the pinnacle in training and very specialized (see Chapter Seven). The standard of work seen at trials is exceptionally high, and success for the participants has been achieved only by years of dedication and specialized breeding. Many have graduated from working tests, the nursery training school for up and coming dogs of people like gamekeepers.

GUIDE DOGS FOR THE BLIND

Besides the many pleasurable pursuits that Labradors can be involved in, it is well-known that they make excellent guide dogs for unsighted people.

UK

The British breeding centre produces many future guide dogs and brood bitches — in fact, about 200 bitches and 40 stud dogs, many of whom live in private homes, under the supervision of the centre.

At six weeks of age the puppies are placed in the homes of puppy walkers, where they live as part of the family unit for nine to twelve months. They take part in complete family life, from visiting schools and shops, to rambles in the country. Once a month they are each visited by a trained member of the guide dog staff, who will discuss the puppy's progress, and iron out any problems that the puppy walker may have encountered.

Between the ages of ten and twelve months the puppies are returned to their respective centres for assessment. They are stringently tested for character, correct and biddable temperament and intelligence, and must meet high physical standards which will be needed to assist blind owners. If the dog passes the tests, it begins serious training for five months, and this is when the public sees the dogs being brought into the local town daily for town traffic instruction.

Below: *Guide dogs for the blind must learn to guide their owners to the correct bus stop, sit and wait patiently for the bus to arrive, then guide their owners onto the bus and to a seat.*

· After training a guide dog will be introduced to its future owner, who will spend about a month living at the centre to learn how to handle and care for the dog, and for the dog to get to know and work with its new owner.

The Guide Dog Association breeds it own stock, which has proved to be so successful that today there is a great demand for them from guide dog schools in many parts of the world as foundation stock.

A great deal of work has gone into cross-breeding, in what has been a very successful effort to find

Above: *This young Labrador bitch is being given pavement training in a busy town. She is taught to stop and sit when she approaches the edge of the pavement.*

Right: *Once she has learned to sit on reaching the kerb, she must then watch and listen for traffic, discouraging her owner from crossing until the road is clear.*

the precise temperament that will ultimately qualify a guide dog, fulfilling the need for a kind, sensitive and willing dog. The

Golden Retriever male, mated to a Labrador female, has proved to be the most successful, followed by the Curly-coated Retriever to the Labrador, and the working Collie to the Golden Retriever.

USA

The 'Seeing Eye' has its headquarters in San Raphael, near San Francisco, California, where the dogs are housed in purpose-built buildings, with expert trainers on hand. The involvement of the public is encouraged and volunteers go, once a week, to groom, weigh and generally condition and socialize puppies from six weeks of age, acquainting them with minor traffic conditions within the grounds.

These puppies stay within the establishment for three months, before being selected for places in individual puppy walkers' homes, by which time a detailed picture of each puppy has been charted.

The future guide dog owners stay with their selected dog until they are confident they can take their guides to live at their own homes with them.

Scattered throughout the United States are ten more guide dog schools, all independent of each other, and totally unconnected. Each has to supply its own funding and dogs.

PAT DOGS

A member dog-owner of the PAT Dogs organisation has a temperament test done on his or her dog, and after acceptance as a PAT Dog a registration disc is issued. This entitles dog and owner, by prior arrangement, to visit selected establishments, such as homes for the aged, the physically disabled, mentally handicapped, and some hospitals and other institutions.

The therapeutic value of contact between dogs and patients and staff, thus creating a more normal

Below: *Lucas is an old hand as a PAT Dog; he is calm and gentle, sitting quietly while patients stroke him and talk to him on his visits to the local hospitals and invalid homes.*

atmosphere in an institutional environment, is incalculable. Everyone working and living in residences and hospital units where PAT Dogs has been accepted derives great emotional and mental stimulation from it.

HEARING DOGS FOR THE DEAF

A recently formed charity takes rescue dogs of various suitable breeds and cross-breeds and socializes them, training them to everyday sounds and to alert their deaf owners. A baby could be crying for example, and the hearing dog would draw its deaf mother's attention to it.

SNIFFER DOGS

Usually trained by the police, army or air force, and frequently seen at airports accompanying customs officials searching luggage, sniffer dogs can detect drugs and ammunition. Labradors and other gundogs have been found to be very suitable for this type of work.

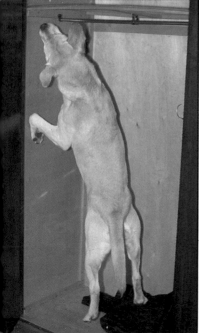

Above: *Dogs are trained by the Royal Army Veterinary Corps to detect hidden explosives. Their excellent sense of smell makes them ideal for this type of work.*

Opposite: *Highly trained police dogs use their acute sense of smell to sniff out drugs concealed in homes or luggage at airports.*

Left: *Labradors are diligent workers, and will search high and low for hidden objects, whether in homes, cars, trains or airports.*

DEVASTATION RESCUE TEAMS

Trained Labradors and Golden Retrievers are often used after a disaster such as an earthquake or bomb devastation to search among the ruins where humans are not agile enough to tread. The dogs are trained to scent out human bodies and to bark if they discover buried people.

Chapter Eight

WORKING, FIELD AND AGILITY TESTS AND TRIALS

Working tests
Field trials
Working trials
Agility tests

WORKING TESTS

Many labrador owners derive satisfaction from the challenge of training their dog as a working gundog during the summer. Socially, weekly meetings are fun, and the dogs certainly enjoy learning basic obedience the natural way.

Membership of a local gundog or breed society is required, and among the fraternity will be found people who are involved in field trials, and gamekeepers bringing on new puppies, as well as many very helpful working test enthusiasts. Besides basic obedience, the dogs learn to scent, hunt and retrieve, both on land and in water.

Graduating from obedience training to the novice working test, held under Kennel Club rules, and staged by local clubs, the dogs take proficiency tests that require them to sit steadily in line with other dogs, move in line at heel and off the lead, sit and be steady to gunshot, mark and retrieve fallen dummies and retrieve only when asked, and bring the dummy straight back to hand.

Having proved themselves, they will be able to advance to intermediate and working tests, which are simulated field trials, using dead pigeons and rabbits. Those who become really interested may be able to take part during the season in winter 'beating' and 'picking up' at local shoots, under

Below: *A Labrador being trained to sit with the dummy that it has just retrieved until the trainer takes it from its mouth.*

the guidance of the gamekeeper belonging to that particular shoot.

Improving with experience, they may be invited to attend at bigger syndicate shoots, but this will happen only after training with the dog for one or two seasons.

Top: *Labradors are trained to jump into the water from a river bank to retrieve a marked bird floating with the current.*

Above: *The Labrador must also learn to retrieve rabbit and heavy hare, for which it must be well built with a strong neck.*

FIELD TRIALS

Field trials are held under kennel club rules during the shooting season. The land is normally surrounded by woodland, and has previously been stocked with pheasant and partridge carefully bred and reared during the previous summer by gamekeepers. Some land, of course, has water and wild fowl as well for the dogs' and handlers' skills to be tested. Great care has to be taken by all present, avoiding disturbing the game at all costs, and ensuring all dogs are under total control.

The breed society holding the trial supplies three judges, licenced by the Kennel Club to judge at various levels from novice trial to the two-day open qualifying stakes.

A trial is a very exciting experience, but it is arduous for some, and those attending must be prepared to do a lot of walking in rough weather over ploughed and rough ground and over thick undergrowth — and they must always obey the spectators steward, who carries a flag and walks up the side of the field level with the line of competitors.

Qualifying certificate

To prove that show dogs in the gundog group are capable of retrieving, a test for a qualifying certificate can either be held by a breed club, or any interested owners can enter their dogs at a field trial and have them tested by qualified judges during the trial, provided they have won one or more challenge certificates at a championship show.

The requirements are that the dog will be steady to gunfire, retrieve fur or feather over land or water, and will retrieve to hand. A certificate enables owners to give their dog its full champion title — provided it has already become a show champion (see Chapter Five).

Quartering

Among the many disciplines a dog must learn during its training to retrieve is to learn to go directly without stopping to the area where the bird has fallen, and to learn to scent it out by 'quartering' to and fro. When the dog picks up the bird, it must try to pick it up by its body and carry it very gently straight back to its handler without being distracted. The reason for returning the bird to 'hand' is so that the handler can take it from the dog's mouth immediately. Otherwise, it could drop a bird that is not quite dead, which may then run away

under cover and die slowly from its wounds.

This is a major reason for employing the retriever.

WORKING TRIALS

Working trials are a popular sport in the United Kingdom and one in which the Labrador, as a breed, performs very successfully.

Companion dog

The lowest stake is CD (Companion Dog) which consists of a fairly testing round of obedience, including heel work on and off the lead, a sendaway to a given point, a

retrieve, a two-minute sit and a ten-minute down, with the handler out of sight. There is also a search for three small articles carrying a stranger's scent and jumps which are the same for all stakes. For a dog over 16in (40cm) at the shoulder, there is a 6ft (2m) scale jump, which has to be negotiated both ways, the dog staying on the other side until recalled by the handler; and a 9ft (3m) long jump, consisting of five sloping boards. To qualify CDEx a dog must attain 80 per cent overall and not less than 70 per cent on any section. In practice, this means that if a dog makes a major mistake, such as failing the scale jump or

Above: *Skill in picking up and returning a bird to hand is learnt by experience; the bird must not be marked or punctured by the dog's teeth.*

coming out in the down, it has no chance of qualifying.

Utility Dog (UD)

The first stake involving a track is UD (Utility Dog). The other exercises are similar to obedience, except that the search consists of four articles in a larger area, and there is a steadiness to gunfire test. The track is at least half an hour old and half a

---

Summary of exercise in Working Trials

Heelwork Performed both on and off the lead, this is to test the dog's ability to remain in the correct position. The dog stands on the handler's left hand side with its shoulder level with the handler's knee, and in this position must undergo a series of turns and halts, with commands and signals being kept to a minimum.

Sit- and down-stay Sit-stays of two minutes duration and down-stays of 10 minutes duration are performed, either in groups or singly. The handler must go to the place indicated by the judge until told to return. Meanwhile, the dog must remain in the sit or down position until released by the handler.

Recall to handler The dog is recalled from the sit or down position. The handler is instructed by the judge to stand at a given distance from the dog, and on the command of heel the dog must return to the handler at a brisk pace and sit in front of him.

Retrieve a dumb-bell The handler throws a dumb-bell as instructed by the judge. On command, the dog must move to retrieve the object, and on further command must return to present it to the handler, sitting in front of him to do so.

Send away and directional command The dog must confidently go away from the handler to a required distance, up to 50yd (46m) according to the test, and may be required to obey re-directional commands given by the handler at the behest of the judge.

Steadiness to gun-fire The dog may be on or off the lead while the gun is discharged, and excited barking, signs of fear or aggressive behaviour will be penalized.

Speak on command The dog is ordered to speak and cease

speaking on command, and may be in the sit or down position according to the handler's discretion.

Agility scale jump The dog is required to scramble over the scale jump, the height of which is determined by the height of the dog at the shoulder — the height being 3ft (almost 1m) for dogs not exceeding 10in (25cm) at the shoulder, 4ft (1.2m) for dogs not exceeding 15in (38cm), and 6ft (1.8m) for dogs exceeding 15in at the shoulder. The dog and handler must approach the scale at a walking pace and halt at a determined distance. The dog is then ordered to scale the jump and on reaching the other side must stay in the down, sit or stand position as previously elected by the handler. The dog should then remain steady until recalled by the handler.

Agility clear and long jumps Except for smaller breeds, under 15in (38cm) in height, the clear jump usually consists of a 3ft (1m) high hurdle which the dog must clear from a standing start. The long jump is usually 9ft (2.7m) long for larger breeds, also taken from a standing start. The handler may approach these jumps with the dog or may stand by the jumps and command the dog to jump. Once the dog has cleared a jump it should remain steady on the other side until joined by the handler.

Searching The dog is required to search an area 15yd (14m) square or 25yd (23m) square according to the test being taken. Three or four articles are positioned in the area and the dog must locate two of them to qualify. A time limit of four or five minutes is given to this exercise.

Tracking On the day prior to the trial, the steward lays the track, which may be a single line or include turns. The dog must follow the track and find the well-scented articles which have been left there.

mile (800m) long, and can be laid in quite a complicated pattern. There is a post to mark the start of the track and another mark 30 yards (27m) on, to indicate the direction of the start. After that the dog and handler are on their own and the latter has to rely on the former. There is an article to be found at the end of the track.

Tracking Dog (TD) and Police Dog (PD)

One of the two stakes is TD (Tracking Dog). All Labradors that have become working trial champions have done so by winning two TD stakes. The track is at least three hours old and has three articles

Left: *A simulated gundog trial at Crufts Dog Show, London in 1987, where experienced working Labradors displayed their range of impressive skills — searching, tracking and retrieving.*

on it, two of which the dog must find in order to qualify. The other senior stake is PD (Police Dog) which involves criminal (man) work. Although a few Labradors have been trained for this stake, to the best of my knowledge none have ever won it.

There have been many successful Labradors in working trials, and there are currently quite a number working their way up the stakes. As they have such wonderful noses and are such highly co-operative dogs, they are extremely well suited to the work involved, with the possible exception of the obedience section, in which they are usually adequate rather than brilliant. The jumps do not normally present any serious difficulties until the Labradors are eight or nine years old.

USA

Working titles

These tests are designed to reward the best working retrievers with certificates and titles of recognition. They add another dimension of competition for the retriever owner, and also provide a standardized evaluation of the dogs' working abilities. Breeders can prove the retrieving and game-finding ability of their dogs through these hunting tests. These achievements are not at the moment recognized by the AKC.

Field trial titles recognised by the AKC

The purpose of a non-slip retriever trial is to determine the relative merits of retrievers in the field. Field (FC) or amateur field championship (AFC) titles signify the pinnacle in this competition. These are, of course, different stakes geared to the performance of the individual dog.

The 'Derby' is for dogs over six months and under two years of age, 'qualifying' is for dogs that have never won a place in an all-age stake, and 'open to all' is for all dogs.

National Open and National Amateur Retriever Championship Stakes earn the winner the title of

field or amateur field trial champion. A dual champion will have its title in the field and on the bench as well.

The field trials themselves are somewhat different in procedure from a trial held in the UK. Because there is a lack of game, dead birds are usually placed unseen for the dogs, who usually retrieve three birds, one of which may be live — but which will have been penned and released over the area precipitating a live bird, at a signalled moment.

A system of 'honouring' is encouraged, to promote steadiness, when the last dog to retrieve has to sit near the next participant while it

marks its falling bird. More emphasis is put on water work too, and training for these field trials is extremely professional.

AGILITY

Labradors have a natural ability and love for agility, only recently introduced as a competitive sport in the United Kingdom. Agility has since become increasingly popular in other parts of the world. Many of the obstacles used in agility today have been used in the past by the police, the Royal Air Force and certain dog training clubs for demonstrations.

Above: *Obedience trials in the USA include exercises similar to those involved in working trials in the United Kingdom, only here dogs must learn to retrieve over jumps as well as on the flat. Many points are lost if the dog drops the dumb-bell while jumping.*

Agility tests were first introduced at the Crufts Dog Show in 1978, where dogs competed against the clock, using a method of faulting. The sport was legalized by the British Kennel Club in 1980 and a set of rules was set up. These do vary in other countries of the world. See the box opposite for a list of the various obstacles which a dog must get over, under or through during the course of the competition. Owners keen to participate in the sport should join the Agility Club, a club in the UK that has a worldwide membership.

Agility tests are becoming increasingly popular at local agricultural shows, as well as having become a major feature at Crufts Dog show in London. Few dogs reach this standard of ability — the German Shepherd Dog excels at the sport — but it is a very exciting spectacle.

It must be remembered that the

Below: *A Labrador negotiating the weaving poles in an agility test. Once a dog has learnt the art of agility, it eagerly looks forward to taking part in it.*

Agility tests

handlers must also be fit to take part in agility tests, since they are required to run alongside the dog throughout the course.

Training

Extensive control over your dog at a distance is essential before starting to teach agility. A Labrador can be taught to negotiate a jump or 'A'-frame by the trainer and dog doing it together first for a few times. With repetition, plenty of encouragement and patience, you can soon give the animal the confidence it needs to perform the exercises spontaneously.

A Labrador's prime aim is to please its owner or handler, so it is essential to end any period of training when the dog has achieved some degree of success. If the dog cannot clear a jump, make it lower so that it can, and praise lavishly.

Schedule of Agility Tests

Agility Tests — Courses and Obstacles

The following obstacles meet with the approval of the Committee of the Kennel Club but organisers may submit others for approval if desired. No practice is to be allowed on the course.

1 **Test Area** The test area must measure not less than 40 yards x 30 yards and have a non-slip surface.

2 **Course** A minimum of ten and a maximum of 18 comprise a test course.

3 **Obstacles**

Hurdle: Height 2ft 6in maximum. Width: 4ft 0in minimum.

Dog Walk: Height: 4ft 0in minimum, 4ft 6in maximum. Walk plank width: 8in minimum, 12in maximum. Length: 12ft 0in minimum, 14ft 0in maximum. Ramps to have anti-slip slats at intervals to be firmly fixed to top plank.

Hoop: Aperture diameter: 1ft 3in minimum. Aperture centre from ground 3ft 0in maximum.

Brush Fence: Dimensions as for hurdle.

Table: Surface: 3ft 0in square minimum. Height: 3ft 0in maximum. To be of stable construction with non-slip surface.

Collapsible Tunnel: Diameter: 2ft 0in minimum, 2ft 6in maximum. Length: 12ft 0in. Circular of non-rigid material construction with entrance of rigid construction and fixed or weighted to the ground.

'A' ramp: Length: 3 yards minimum, 3⅔ yards maximum. Width: 3ft 0in. Height of apex from ground 6ft 3in. Two ramps hinged at apex. Surface of ramps slatted at intervals.

Weaving Poles: Number 6 minimum, 12 maximum. Distance apart 2ft 0in maximum.

Pipe Tunnel: Diameter: 2ft minimum. Length: 10ft 0in minimum.

See-Saw: Width: 8in minimum, 12in maximum. Length: 12ft 0in minimum, 14ft 0in maximum. Height of central bracket from ground, 2ft 3in maximum. A plank firmly mounted on central bracket.

Long-jump: Length: 5ft maximum. Width: 4ft minimum. Height: 1ft maximum.

Pause Box: Defined area 4ft x 4ft.

Marking
Standard Marking

5 faults for each failure to negotiate any obstacle correctly.
Failure to correctly complete the course — disqualified.

Other marking

Any form of marking other than 'Standard' must be stated in the schedule.

Appendix

Major kennel clubs

Australia Australian National Kennel Council, Royal Show Grounds, Ascot Vale, Victoria (Incorporating: The Canine Association of Western Australia; North Australian Canine Association; The Canine Control Council (Queensland); Canberra Kennel Association; The Kennel Control Council; Kennel Control Council of Tasmania; The RAS Kennel Club; South Australian Canine Association)
Canada Canadian Kennel Club, 2150 Bloor Street West, Toronto M6S 1M8, Ontario
France Societe Centrale Canine, 215 Rue St Denis, 75083 Paris, Cedex 02
Germany Verband für das Deutsche Hundewesen (VDH), Postfach 1390, 46 Dortmund
New Zealand Kennel Club, Private Bag, Porirua
South Africa Kennel Union of Southern Africa, 6th Floor, Bree Castle, 68 Bree Street, Cape Town 8001, S. Africa, PO Box 11280, Vlaeberg 8018
United Kingdom The Kennel Club, 1-4 Clarges Street, London W1Y 8AB
United States of America American Kennel Club, 51 Madison Avenue, New York, NY 10010

Breed clubs

United Kingdom
East Anglian Labrador Club, Hon Sec Mrs Kinsella, The Mount, Fingrinhoe, Near Colchester, Essex
Labrador Club of Northern Ireland, Hon Sec A J Kilpatrick, 16 Corby Drive, Lisburn, Co Antrin, Northern Ireland
Labrador Club of Scotland, Hon Sec Mrs A M Pollock, 46 Orchard Street, Galston, Ayrshire KA4 8EL
Labrador Club of Wales, Hon Sec Mr G Howells, 18 Gwernant, Clumllynfell, Swansea, Glamorgan
Midland Counties Labrador Club, Hon Sec Mr F Whitbread, Blackbrook Farm, Mercaston Lane, Near Turnditch, Derby DE5 2LU
Kent Surrey and Sussex Labrador Club, Hon Sec Mrs S Newton, 'Lorchis', 59 Claygate Road, Dorking, Surrey
Northumberland and Durham Labrador Club, Hon Sec Miss E Smith, 29 High Street, Gosforth, Newcastle on Tyne
The Labrador Club, Hon Sec Mrs J Coulson, Broadacre, Broad Lane, Hambledon, Hants
Three Ridings Labrador Club, Hon Sec Mrs M Wilkinson, Wilkamaur Cottage, 33 Brook Street, Adlington, Chorley, Lancashire
Ulster Retriever Club, Hon Sec Mr H A Wilson, Nesfield House, 71 Queensway, Lisburn, Co Antrin, Northern Ireland
United Retriever Club, Hon Sec Mrs P Homes, Moorcraft, Goldcliffe, Newport, Gwent
West of England Labrador Club, Hon Sec Mrs N Leah, Old Orchard, Bounders Lane, Bolangey, Perranporth, Cornwall
Yellow Labrador Club, Hon Sec Mr H W Clayton, Ardmargha Cottage, Bright Hampton, Standlake, Witney, Oxon

United States of America
Labrador Retriever Club, Secretary John W McAssey, Rt 7, Box 912, Tallahassee, FL 32308

Bibliography and further reading

The Retriever Owner's Enclyclopaedia, Pelham Books, London
The Labrador Retriever, Lorna Countess Howe and G Waring, Popular Dogs, London
The Labrador, M Kinsella, Arthur Baker Ltd, London
Gundog Training and Field Trials, P R A Moxon, Popular Dogs, London
Training the Rough Shooter's Dog, P R A Moxon, Popular Dogs, London
All About the Labrador Retriever, M Roslin-Williams, Pelham Books, London
The Dual Purpose Labrador, M Roslin-Williams, Pelham Books, London
The Complete Labrador Retriever, H Warwick, Howell Book House, New York
Dogs: Their Mating, Whelping and Weaning, K White, K & R Books
A Dog of Your Own, J Palmer, Salamander Books Ltd, London
Training Your Dog, J Palmer, Salamander Books Ltd, London
Dogs and How To Breed Them, Hilary Harmer, Gifford, UK
The Evans Guide for Counseling Dog Owners, Job Michael Evans, Howell Book House Inc, New York
Happy Dog/Happy Owner, M Siegal, Howell Book House Inc, New York

Useful addresses

The United Kingdom
The Agility Club The Spinney, Aubrey Lane, Redbourn, Hertfordshire AL3 7AN
Battersea Dogs Home 4 Battersea Park Road, Battersea, London SW8 4AA
The Blue Cross Animals Hospital, 1 High Street, Victoria, London SW1V 1QQ
British Field Sports Society 59 Kennington Road, London SE1 7PZ
British Small Animals Veterinary Association 7 Mansfield Street, London W1M 0AT
British Veterinary Association 7 Mansfield Street, London W1M 0AT
Groomers Association 4th Floor, Onslow House, 60-66 Saffron Hill, London EC1N 8QX
The Guide Dogs for the Blind Association 9-11 Park Street, Windsor, Berkshire SL4 1JR
Hearing Dogs for the Deaf 105 Gower Street, London WC1
Joint Advisory Committee on Pets in Society Walter House, 418-422 The Strand, London WC2
National Canine Defence League 1 Pratt Mews, London NW1 0AD
National Dog Owners' Association 39-41 North Road, Islington, London N7 9DP
People's Dispensary for Sick Animals PDSA House, South Street, Dorking, Surrey
Pet Food Manufacturers' Association 6 Catherine Street, London WC2B 5JJ
Pet Trade and Industry Association 4th Floor, Onslow House, 60-66 Saffron Hill, London EC1N 8QX
PRO Dogs Rocky Bank, New Road, Ditton, Maidstone, Kent ME20 6AD
The Royal Society for the Prevention of Cruelty to Animals RSPCA Headquaraters, Causeway, Horsham, Sussex RH12 1HG

United States of America
American Animal Hospital Association 3612 East Jefferson, South Bend, Indiana 46615
American Humane Association (incorporating The Hearing Dog Association) 5351 Roslyn, Denver, Colorado 80201
American Society for the Prevention of Cruelty to Animals 441 East 92nd Street, New York, New York 10028
American Veterinary Medical Association 930 North Meacham Road, Schaumburg, Illinois 60196
Animal Welfare Institute PO Box 3650, Washington D.C. 20007
The Fund for Animals 140 West 57th Street, New York, New York 10019
Guide Dogs for the Blind PO Box 1200, San Rafael, California 94902
The Humane Society of the United States 2100 L Street, N.W., Washington D.C. 20037
International Association of Pet Cemeteries 27 West 150 North Avenue, West Chicago, Illinois 60185
Leader Dogs for the Blind 1039 South Rochester Road, Rochester, Michigan 48063
National Dog Groomers Association PO Box 101, Clark, Pennsylvania 16113
The National Dog Registry 227 Stebbins Road, Carmel, New York 1051
Orthopaedic Foundation for Animals 817 Virginia Avenue, Columbia, Missouri 65201
Owner Handler Association of America 583 Knoll Court, Seaford, New York 11783
Pet Food Institute 1101 Connecticut Avenue N.W., Washington D.C. 200326
The Seeing Eye Inc 100 East Kilgore Road, Kalamazoo, Michigan 49001

Glossary of dog terminology

Angulation: Angle formed by the bones, mainly the shoulder, forearm, stifle and hock.

Anorchid: Male animal without testicles.

Anus: Anterior opening under the tail.

Backline: Topline of dog from neck to tail.

Bitch: Female dog.

Breastbone: Bone running down the middle of the chest, to which all but the floating ribs are attached; sternum.

Brisket: The forepart of the body below the chest between the forelegs.

Brood bitch: Female used for breeding.

Bull neck: A heavy neck, well-muscled.

Canine: Animal of the genus canis which includes dogs, foxes, wolves and jackals.

Canines: The four large teeth in the front of the mouth, two upper and two lower next to incisors.

Carpals: Bones of the pastern joints.

Castrate: To surgically remove the testes of a male.

Cow-hocked: Hocks turned inwards.

Croup: The rear part of the back above the hind legs.

Crown: The highest part of the head: the top of the skull.

Cryptorchid: A male dog with neither testicle descended.

Cull: To eliminate unwanted puppies.

Dam: Mother of the puppies.

Dew claw: Extra claw on the inside lower portion of legs.

Dome: The rounded part of the skull.

Entropion: A condition in which the eyelid turns inward and the lashes irritate the eyeball.

Femur: The large heavy bone of the thigh between the pelvis and stifle joint.

Flank: Side of the body between the last rib and the hip.

Forearm: Front leg between elbow and pastern.

Foreface: Front part of the head before the eyes; the muzzle.

Hare foot: A long narrow foot.

Haw: A third eyelid at the inside corner of the eye.

Heat: An alternative word for 'season' in bitches.

Heel: Command by handler to keep the dog close to his heel.

Heel free: Command whereby the dog must walk to heel without a lead.

Height: Vertical measurements from withers to ground.

Hie on: A command to urge the dog on used in hunting or Field trials.

Hip dysplasia: Malformation of the ball of the hip joint; usually hereditary.

Hock: Lower joint of the hindlegs.

Hucklebones: Top of the hip bones.

Humerus: Bone of the upper arm.

In-breeding: The mating of closely related dogs of the same standard.

Incisors: Upper and lower front teeth between the canines.

Ischium: Hipbone.

In season: On heat, ready for mating.

Interbreeding: The breeding together of different varieties.

Jowls: Flesh of lips and jaws.

Leather: The flap of the ear.

Level bite: The upper and lower teeth edge to edge.

Line breeding: The mating of related dogs within a line or family to a common ancestor, ie dog to grand-dam or bitch to grand-sire.

Litter: The pups from one whelping.

Loaded: Superfluous muscle.

Loin: Either side of the vertebrae column between the last rib and hip bone.

Mate: The sex act between the dog and bitch.

Milk teeth: First teeth. (Puppies lose these at four to six months.)

Molars: Rear teeth.

Monorchid: A male animal with only one testicle in the scrotum.

Muzzle: The head in front of the eyes, including nose, nostril and jaws.

Nose: The ability to scent.

Occiput: The rear of the skull.

Oestrum: The period during which a bitch has her menstrual flow and can be mated.

Out-crossing: The mating of unrelated individuals of the same breed.

Overshot: Front teeth (incisors) of the upper jaw overlap and do not touch the teeth of the lower jaw.

Pads: The tough, cushioned soles of the feet.

Paper foot: A flat foot with thin pads.

Pastern: Foreleg between the carpus and the digits.

Patella: Knee cap composed of cartilage at the stifle joint.

Pelvis: Set of bones attached to the end of the spinal column.

Puppy: A dog up to 12 months of age.

Quarters: The two hindlegs.

Scapula: The shoulder blade.

Scissor bite: The outside of the lower incisors touches the inner side of the upper incisors.

Second thigh: The part of the hindquarters from the stifle to hock.

Set on: Insertion or attachment of tail or ears.

Set up: Posed so as to make the most of the dog's appearance for the show ring.

Sire: A dog's male parent.

Snipy: Muzzle pointed and weak.

Soft-mouthed: Able to carry retrieved game in the mouth without damaging it.

Spay: To surgically remove the ovaries to prevent conception.

Splay feet: Feet with toes spread wide.

Stake: A competition held at a Field Trial.

Stern: Tail of a sporting dog or hound.

Sternum: The brisket or breast bone.

Stifle: The hindlegs above the hock.

Stop: Indentation between the eyes.

Stud: Male used for breeding.

Sway back: A sagging back.

Tail set: How the base of the tail sets on the rump.

Thigh: Hindquarters from hip to stifle.

Throatiness: An excess of loose skin under the throat.

Topline: The dog's outline from just behind the withers to the tail set.

Turn-up: An up-tilted foreface.

Undershot: The front teeth of the lower jaw projecting or overlapping the front teeth of the upper jaw.

Upper arm: The humerus or bone of the foreleg between shoulder blade and the forearm.

Vent: The anal opening.

Whelp: The act of giving birth.

Wind: To catch the scent of game.

Withers: The highest point of the shoulders just behind the neck.